The Other Side
Of The Nightstick

WILLIAM E. WINDER

authorHOUSE®

AuthorHouse™
1663 Liberty Drive
Bloomington, IN 47403
www.authorhouse.com
Phone: 833-262-8899

Published by AuthorHouse 03/26/2021

ISBN: 978-1-6655-2104-8 (sc)
ISBN: 978-1-6655-2103-1 (e)

Print information available on the last page.

CONTENTS

Dedication vii

Chapter 1   Waking Up in the ICU 1
Chapter 2   Reliving the Trauma 8
Chapter 3   Visiting with Mom and Dad 15
Chapter 4   Straight Talk with the Doctor 19
Chapter 5   Making Progress 23
Chapter 6   Mirror, Mirror 30
Chapter 7   Getting Better, but Will the Dreams
             Ever Stop? 37
Chapter 8   Okay, I'm Here; What Do I Do Now? 52
Chapter 9   Can I Have a Little Privacy? 56
Chapter 10   Finally, a Shower 61
Chapter 11   Okay, so I'm Not Superman 68
Chapter 12   Healing 76
Chapter 13   Home at Last 85
Chapter 14   No Longer a Police Officer? 92

Chapter 15   Reliving the Story 102

Chapter 16   Ceremonies and Awards Are Nice,
             but They Don't Pay the Bills...................108

Epilogue.. 115

Back inside cover...121

About the Author 123

DEDICATION

I dedicate this book to the following:

My beautiful and wonderful wife, Bonnie. She has been my light of salvation at the end of a long black tunnel. She has taught me so much about myself and has helped me to change for the good. She holds me late at night when the demons come. She has stood by me and loved and put up with me through all the rough times, and I am, by far, not the easiest person in the world to get along with. She is the reason my heart beats.

My daughter, Elizabeth, and my grandson, Taven. They put a smile on my face, and I love them. I admire my daughter so much for her love and patience in raising my grandson. I love going to visit with them and spending time with them. I thank them for being there for me and standing by me.

My good friend Howard Goldin, former chief of police of Spring Valley, Rockland County, New York. He served with the US Army in Vietnam from June 1967 to July 1968, in the 4th Battalion, 23rd Infantry Division, rank of Spec 5. He was wounded in combat four times. He has helped me learn that giving both time and effort is a wholesome thing.

He convinced me to join Rotary International with Spring Valley, New York, and I have learned that service above self is the most important thing in life. He has been there for me as a friend and a brother. A patient and compassionate man, he has helped me through some very rough times. I love and respect him.

My good friend Edward Frank, former assistant general manager, maintenance support, MaBSTOA May 1973 to June 2006. He served in the US Navy in Vietnam from November 1969 to November 1970, River Ron Assault Division 152 aboard ATC49, what we call the Brown Water Navy, with the rank of Seaman E-3. Ed has been there for me for many years, has guided me down the right paths, and has helped me to make good decisions. Respect.

My friend Roy Tschudy, a former NYC police officer. He served in the US Army in Vietnam from January 1968 through February 1969 in the 271st Aviator Group, 1st Aviator Brigade, rank Spec 4. We served next to each other for years on the job as police officers and never knew we were both Vietnam veterans. He is an amazing friend with a huge heart.

A special thank-you to Mr. William Greenleaf of Greenleaf Literary Services for all the help and direction he gave me in preparing this book. A fantastic writer, freelance editor, book doctor, and ghostwriter. Thank you, Bill.

My brother and sister veterans, especially my Vietnam Veterans of America pals. It was you who saved my life and my sanity when I surely would have lost both. Regardless of what I was going through, and making others go through, you stood at my shoulder and steered me the right way.

And to all the other police officers out there who put

on a uniform and wear the shield or badge. Those who live the job day in and day out, 365 days a year, who aren't allowed to bring their personal life or problems onto the job. Those the public doesn't see as human beings, but rather as a necessary evil, someone to do the job, to work all hours, all weather, all holidays, to do a job the people themselves don't have the guts or temperament to do. God bless you all and keep you safe. I write this book so the public can get some idea of how we're treated and how we live, and for me, what it's like living with the pain and disappointment of being shot on duty.

If my getting shot in the face was instrumental in providing the much-needed bulletproof vests and all the protection and equipment they need to do the job safely, then it was worth all the pain and the nightmares.

CHAPTER 1

Waking Up in the ICU

M Y EYES OPEN, AND THROUGH the blur, I notice I'm in a large white room. Long white florescent lights hang from the ceiling. Inside the plastic covers are bodies of dead flies. The smell of rubbing alcohol and old urine wafts through the air. The wall clock reads 3:10 p.m. In the corner is a counter with nurses working at their desks. A uniformed police officer stands over me next to my bed, holding my hand. On his left shoulder, I read the familiar patch: *New York City Transit Police*. Although barely conscious, I immediately recognize the face of the officer wearing that patch.

He sees that I'm awake, and tears well in his eyes. His name is Richie Donalan, but he's known as "Scotty" to all of us who work with him. A seasoned veteran police officer, Scotty taught me the dos and don'ts of policing as a young rookie. He broke me into the job.

I attempt to speak, but no voice comes out.

When I realize I can't speak, panic seeps in. I try to sit

up, but I can't. Something is holding me down. I get scared, and as I wrestle, Scotty tries to hold me down.

A nurse runs over and places her hands gently over mine. Her voice is calm, yet also direct. "You're very sick," she says. "I'm going to explain some things to you, but you must remain still."

I nod that I understand.

"The reason you can't speak," she continues, "is because you have a tracheotomy tube in your throat to help you breathe."

My mind's eye pictures what my throat must look like. What the hell happened to me?

She notices I'm getting upset. "Don't worry. When they take the tube out, it'll heal up and you'll be as good as new."

I know she's trying to help calm me down and make me feel better, but I find little comfort in her words.

"You also have ice packs around your neck and throat to take down the swelling."

As she continues to talk, a dull, throbbing pain seems to take root and grow in my neck and throat. My mouth feels dry, and I move my tongue to moisten it. I can hardly feel my tongue, and I can't feel the inside of my mouth. My tongue glides over my teeth, and I realize that several are missing and some others are cut in half. Although I can't feel my tongue, I can sense the taste of blood in my mouth.

The nurse continues to talk in her soothing voice. "You have IV tubes in both of your arms and an electrocardiogram hooked up to your chest, so please be still or you'll hurt yourself more. A feeding tube is inserted in your nose, and that runs down to your stomach. Last, but certainly not least, you have a tube in your penis to help you drain urine."

I nod once again. I'm aware that Scotty has moved back out of the way.

"If you need anything, just tap on the side rail of the bed and write it down on this pad." She places the pad of paper and a pen next to me on the bed.

I pick it up and write, *Why can't I feel my mouth and tongue?*

"Your doctor will be here soon and explain everything to you. Now try and get some sleep."

As she turns and walks away, I realize that I'm breathing but not through my mouth or nose. I think hard about this realization of not being able to breathe on my own and not being able to speak, and I again panic. I try to rise up and move my arms. My eyes fill with tears as I envision myself having to breathe through this tube for the rest of my life. As the tears come, my nasal passage starts to leak, my throat fills up, and I begin to choke. I can't breathe, and I panic more.

Two nurses run over. One holds me while the other puts on latex gloves. She grabs a plastic hose from a bag and a plastic attachment for the end and starts to suction out the tracheotomy tube. The nurse holding me soothes me as this is performed. The feeling of the suction tube being snaked around my throat reminds me of how a repairman cleans out a pipe. When they're done, the inside of my throat feels raw and sore. I'm exhausted. My eyes close, and I drift off to sleep.

★ ★ ★

Suddenly, I become aware that I'm in a rocky area covered by trees and high grass. I hear the distinct sound of rifle fire around me. I realize that I'm in a hot landing zone in the Que

Son Valley in South Vietnam, and we're taking fire from three sides. I'm on the ground, firing outward while lying next to our machine gunner, Troy. He's from St. Albans, New York. The lieutenant is on the radio barking out commands and fire mission coordinates.

The firing goes on for what seems like forever. Our squad leader, Eddie, who's from Maryland, takes a round in the right shoulder. The round comes out his back, along with pieces of meat and clothing. We call for the corpsman (a navy medic assigned to marine units), and he crawls up and starts to work on Eddie. I crawl to a large boulder by Troy and look for a muzzle flash in the distance. I see a number of flashes, and I start firing in that direction. Troy opens up with his M60 machine gun, and empty shell casings begin landing on top of me. They're real hot as they leave the chamber and burn as they hit my skin and bounce off. I tell myself to never take a firing position to the right of the machine gun again.

Right away, we hear the all-too-familiar sound of a Huey helicopter. Two choppers fly past us and head forward to the hill where the enemy fire is coming from. The choppers fly in, and as they make their descent, they fire rockets at the hill area around us, setting off tremendous explosions as the rockets find the targets. The firing stops, and everything is quiet.

Troy pats me on the back. "We fooled them again, Bill. They can't kill us. We're too mean."

As I pick myself up, I respond, "I don't know about that killing stuff. They keep trying real hard, and it gets harder and harder to stay alive around here."

I press the magazine release latch on my M16 rifle, and the empty magazine drops down. I take a full magazine, tap it on my helmet to assure that all the rounds are seated correctly, then slip it up into the rifle and let the bolt go home, chambering the first round. We look up and wave as the Hueys fly back the way they came. I grab my canteen and take a long swallow. The water is hot, and it tastes like chlorine from a pool because of the halazone tablets we have to treat it with to keep bacteria out.

I close my eyes and try to think of home, the real world.

★ ★ ★

I'm back in my bed in the ICU ward at the hospital. My eyes search the room to access my surroundings. Walls are painted a rough cream color with black marks on them where it's obvious they've been struck by rolling beds. No windows. About eight beds as far as I can tell. All full. Staff running around trying to bring comfort to the people who've been victimized by a crime-ridden neighborhood or who are just sick.

Scotty grabs my hand and squeezes it. He looks toward the door. My wife and sister-in-law are walking toward my bed. With them is a short, well-dressed Black man I've never seen before. As they come closer, I take a long look at my wife's face. It's drawn and worried. Her eyes are all red and swollen. Scotty gives my hand a squeeze and steps back from the bed. My wife leans over and kisses me gently on my cheek. I can't help but think to myself that her smile seems forced and not at all natural.

My sister-in-law leans down and kisses me too. "Hi, sweetheart. We all miss you, and everyone says hi."

My wife says, "I love you so much, honey. You have to stay still so you can get better and I can take you home."

I can't understand why my wife doesn't grab me and hug me close. She's usually a very emotional woman. I feel sad and overwhelmed. I feel like crying. My eyes water, and my throat begins to fill up. I start to choke and reach out for air.

The Black man steps forward and grabs my arm. I notice his blue suit and tie underneath his open white jacket. He holds my arm, and I see that his fingers are manicured and slim.

"Look at my face," he says. "Listen to my words. Don't get upset. You still have a lot of blood and mucous in your throat and chest. If you get upset, you'll cry. That will clog your tube, and you won't be able to breathe."

The dull, throbbing pain in my throat and neck is getting worse, and I now start to be aware of many painful spots in my throat and face. I always thought I could stand high degrees of pain. All my years in karate and my years in the Marine Corps and Vietnam had toughened me up. I had had quite a few fights, both in the ring and on the streets of the Bronx.

I was no stranger to pain, but I guess the intensity of this pain must have shown on my face.

"What's wrong, sweetheart?" my wife asks.

I point to my throat and shake my head.

The Black man calls over a nurse. She arrives with a hypodermic needle. As he talks, I become aware of an accent that I've never heard before.

He takes the needle and injects the contents into my right buttock. "This injection won't take away all the pain you're experiencing, I'm sorry to say, but it will make you drowsy and sleepy. Sleep is very important for you because you'll heal with more rest." He pats my arm and walks away, giving the nurses some instructions as he goes.

I point to the man, now reaching the door, look at my wife, and write on my pad, *Who is he?*

"He's one of the doctors who operated on you when you were brought in. He's a cardiovascular surgeon. You were very lucky he was there."

While she's still speaking, I begin slipping off to sleep. I hear her voice echoing in my head as the injection starts to work.

CHAPTER 2

Reliving the Trauma

I'M STANDING UP, HOLDING ON *to a strap on the downtown D Train Express. I'm on my way to work and reading the little advertisement billboards they have on the train. One of them is trying to talk people into taking a test to become a police officer. I tell myself that I can do this. It would be a good job for me, more money for my family: my wife, Peggy, and my newborn daughter, Elizabeth. I write the information down and decide to do it. I'll take the test.*

I get to work and discuss it with a couple of friends. They all tell me I'm crazy. They say nobody ever leaves the company and that I'll probably fail the test.

Suddenly I'm standing in the street, next to some elevated subway stairs. Back then, transit police worked alone. No partner. I'm wearing a dark-blue uniform with a heavy blue overcoat, freshly pressed. In front of me is a blue car. In my hand is my .38-caliber four-inch Smith & Wesson service revolver. I'm pointing it at a tall Black man who is lying facedown on the ground beside the car. The car is parked in front of a bar.

I turn to my left to see two dark figures crouching under the subway stairs. I'm now pointing my revolver at them. Out of the corner of my right eye, I notice movement by the right rear of the car. As I turn to face it, I see a tremendous flash. I feel impact and pain in my neck and throat. I'm lifted into the air and thrown back to the ground. I feel what seems like hundreds of tiny points of burning pain, like hot irons, in my throat and face.

★ ★ ★

I wake up abruptly, kicking my legs and flailing my arms. The pain is unbearable. My throat and face feel like they're on fire. I try to scream, but nothing comes out. *Damn.*

Scotty and two nurses are holding me down so I won't dislodge any of the IV tubes in my arms or the wires in my chest. I finally calm down.

"Jesus, Bill, what the hell scared you like that?" Scotty asks.

I reach for the pad and pen and begin to relate to them on paper what I dreamt about.

"This is just trauma," the nurse says. "It'll pass in time, and you'll learn to live with what happened to you."

When the nurse walks away, I signal Scotty. He turns and looks at me.

I write on my pad, *Why didn't Susan hug me or show more affection when she first saw me?*

Scotty reads what I've written. "She was told by the doctors not to do or say anything that might upset you, or your throat tube would get clogged up. She was doing her very best not to let you see how distressed she really is.

When you fell asleep, she went out in the hallway and cried her eyes out like she's been doing since Monday night when this happened."

Up until now, I hadn't thought about the effect all of this would have on her or the rest of my family. All those years, I knew that this could happen. Every cop does. Yet I still asked her to marry me, and it forced her into going through all of this. I feel selfish, guilty, and terrible about it all. I start to cry. My tube begins to clog, and I gag.

Scotty yells for the nurse, who comes running. She turns on the machine that's positioned on the right side of my bed. Another nurse puts on a pair of surgical gloves. The first nurse takes a long plastic tube from a sealed plastic bag and hooks it up to the machine. She then removes the oxygen tube from my tracheotomy tube and inserts in its place the long, thin plastic hose from the machine. As I feel the tube going down my throat, I gag more because it's so painful. This machine sucks up all the mucous and blood from my throat and around my tube that's blocking my airway.

As the nurse tries to clear my airway, I see my wife and sister-in-law in the far corner of the ICU crying. Scotty is trying to console them and calm them down.

I think to myself, *How long will I have to stay like this? Will I have to spend the rest of my life with these tubes in me? After only six years, is my career as a police officer finished? How can I expect my wife to put up with all of this?* My mind is cluttered with all these thoughts, and being so tired from the tube cleaning, I start to drift off to sleep again.

I feel as if I'm floating in the air. My head is spinning, but the searing pain is still intense. As I slip off into sleep, I can sense the bright lights of the intensive care unit glaring through my eyelids. Despite my overwhelming fear of reliving once more what I've already lived through, my mind dreams again.

★ ★ ★

I find myself lying facedown in the wet and filthy gutter. I try to stand up but find I only have the strength to get to my knees. I look down and see blood all over the street and all over me. There's so much blood. I grab my radio to call for backup and realize that my mouth is full of blood and broken teeth. I speak with a garbled voice into the radio. "Eleven assignment number 74, requesting a 10-13 at 176th Street and Jerome Avenue. Officer down. Shots fired."

There is no acknowledgment to my plea for help. The pain is becoming so bad that it blurs my vision and makes it almost impossible to see anything. I notice my .38-caliber service revolver lying in the street in front of me. I crawl on my hands and knees and pick it up. I look down the street to see four men running wildly away from me. I lift my service revolver and point it at them. They turn the corner and are gone.

I hear a voice yell back, "Remember, man, I'm not the one who shot you."

I also see a crowd of people staring out at me through the bar window. I lift my hands to ask for help, but they stand there in the window, staring at me. Why doesn't someone help me? I did my best to help them. I holster my service weapon.

I crawl to a doughnut shop on the corner. As the man behind the counter sees me, he runs toward me and helps me to a bench. He's talking to me, but I can't hear what he's saying. He's trying to lay me down on the bench, but I fight with him.

I don't want to lie down. I know if I lie down, I'll choke to death on my own blood. He continues to force me to lie down. I start choking because I can't breathe.

* * *

I wake up, gasping and choking for air. The nurses once again begin the process of cleaning out my tube and suctioning the mucus and blood from my throat and airway. My throat and neck are so sore and raw, I'm very glad I can't breathe through my mouth.

When the suctioning is over, one of the nurses pulls a chair up to the bed and sits down next to me. "You had another bad dream, didn't you?"

I nod.

"We have a lot of different drugs here that we can give you: drugs that will make you drowsy, drugs that will put you unconscious, drugs that can dull your pain somewhat. I'm so terribly sorry that we have nothing here that will stop the pain completely or make the dreams go away."

I grab my pad and write, *Do you have any drugs that will make me talk again?*

The nurse reads my note and looks hurt as she rises from her chair. I realize that she was apologizing for not being able to do more for me. She was showing concern and compassion to me, and instead of acknowledging that, I lashed out. As she stands, I grab her arm. She turns and looks at me.

I'm sorry I said that, I write. *It was cruel of me. It's just that I hurt so much, and I'm scared of what's going to happen to me.*

"I understand," she says with a kind smile. "I shouldn't

have been so offended. It's normal for you to be apprehensive, and I wouldn't blame you if you were very bitter toward the people who did this to you. What they did was terrible."

I write, *Well, I haven't had enough time to think about being bitter yet, but give me time.*

While I'm writing, my wife, Susan, and my sister-in-law, Toni, come toward my bed. They both lean over and kiss me and tell me how much they miss me and how the rest of the family loves me and is praying for me to get better and come home. They also tell me that the television news crews want to interview me.

I write, *How can they interview me if I can't talk? I'm not really up to seeing them just yet.* In the back of my mind, I'm thinking, *I don't want anyone to see me like this.*

"Don't worry, sweetheart," Susan says. "They won't see you until you think you're ready for them." She turns to Toni. "Toni, would you excuse Bill and me for a moment, please?"

"Sure, Susie. I'll grab a cigarette out in the hall."

When she's gone, Susie looks at me. "I was speaking to Scotty, and he told me you were disturbed that I didn't hug you like I always do. It's just that after all you've been through, I'm afraid to grab you or upset you in any way for fear of hurting you more. As a matter of fact, we're all having a hard time believing you're still alive after all that."

I write, *I realize that, and Scotty explained to me how much you've been hurting since this happened. Is the job taking good care of you? Where are you staying at night?*

"The Police Benevolent Association has had officers answering phones all night, and they assigned me a driver, Terry Moore, to drive me to and from the hospital. He's been really great to me since this happened. I mean, sometimes he stays with us ten to fourteen hours at a time. His poor wife and daughter hardly get to see him at all. The PBA president, Bill Sullivan, has been handling everything very well so far. He's always asking me if I need anything. I'm staying with Mary and Phil and the kids until you're back home again."

I write, *That's good. At least you're not in the house alone. I want you to know that I love you very much.*

"I have a surprise for you," Susan says, "but you have to promise me you won't get upset."

CHAPTER 3

Visiting with Mom and Dad

WHILE SUSAN TALKS WITH ME, the pain diminishes slightly, though it's by no means gone. It comes back with a vengeance to gnaw agonizingly at my neck and throat until it's unbearable. I grab the side of the bed and point to my neck. Sue gets the nurse's attention, and the nurse runs over. Once again, the needle finds its way into my flesh, and once again, the fluid it contains attempts to give my body a desperate relief from levels of pain I had thought were impossible.

The nurse says, "As we explained to you before, this won't stop all the pain. It will take the edge off and make you drowsy."

I nod. I look at Sue and write, *Where's my surprise?*

"I'll be right back." She hurries toward the hall and motions to someone.

I look toward the doorway and see my mother and father come into the room. My father is a huge man who always appears hard and cold as ice to everyone but is really a gentle soul. His close-cropped hair no longer covers his balding head. My mother, a petite woman only five feet tall and weighing only ninety pounds, is hard as leather from years of shoveling coal into a huge building furnace. Her dull-white hair cascades down her shoulders, and she's wearing an old blue dress. Both of my parents are old before their time and veterans of many heart attacks.

As they get to my bedside, my mother bends down and kisses me on the forehead. My father grabs my hand with his huge, age-spotted fingers and brings it up and kisses it. I notice his unshaven face with the day-old coarse whiskers that always seem to be there. As far back as I can remember, it was as though he always had a day-old beard even when he had just shaved.

My parents have been through everything with me in my life. They've been there for me through school, the Marine Corps, Vietnam, my first marriage, and my joining the police force. I feel so guilty that they have to go through this and see me this way.

"I'm not going to ask you how you feel," my mother says, "because I can see you're in a lot of pain and you have all these tubes and wires coming out of you. We've been sick since we found out about this, but they seem to be taking good care of you here. Do you need anything?"

No! I write. *I'm sorry you have to see me like this.*

"Stop apologizing and get better." By now, tears are streaming down her face, and she's squeezing my hand so hard, I can't feel my fingers.

My father pulls my mother aside and leans in close to me and speaks with his thick Irish accent. "I'm so sad to see you this way, boy, but I'm damn happy you're still alive. You're my son, boy, and I love you like you'll never know.

The doctors tell me you're pretty mangled inside your neck and throat. They had to do a lot of work to pull you through this." Abruptly his voice changes to one of determination. "You have to get out of this job, boy. I cried while you were in Vietnam, and I'm crying now. Please, boy, get out while you still can. Don't be a hero anymore." With that, my father breaks down, and his massive body shakes while he cries.

I write, *I really don't know how bad I'm hurt or how much recovery I'm looking at, but if I quit the job, how will I support my family and pay my bills?*

"Listen to me, lad. You're only twenty-eight years old. You can learn anything you want to do. You're intelligent. Look at your poor wife. You can't take the chance of putting her through this again. You both deserve more from life. You didn't make it home from Vietnam just to get your head almost blown off for helping people who couldn't care if you live or die. You're my son. My only son! I didn't drive a taxi and you mother didn't work as a building superintendent for over thirty years to give you a home, put you through school, and have this happen to you. I won't leave here, boy, until you promise me you'll not go back to that job."

"Archie," my mother says, "you're overstepping your bounds. You have no right to come in here while he's in this condition and make demands on how he lives his life."

I write, *When I decide to get out, it will be mine and Susan's decision. I don't like to talk back to you, Dad, but we haven't had time to think about it yet. After all, I just woke up this morning. Hell, I don't even know how bad this all is or what my face even looks like.*

My father lowers his head and raises his hands to his

face. He takes a long, deep breath and lowers his hands. With tears streaming down his face, he says, "I'm sorry, lad. I just can't stand to see you lying here so helpless and dependent on all these machines, not even able to talk to me. I see your lovely wife here, so drawn and pale. I love this fine girl, and I love you. I really don't mean to tell you what to do. You're right. It's your decision, and I'll trust you to make a good decision, as you always do, boy."

Thanks, Dad, I write. *I know you're worried. Hell, I'll be out of here in no time, and then we can talk about it. Okay? By the way, how did you get here so fast? Did you drive?*

"No, we didn't drive. The police department sent a driver and car and picked us up at home in Rhode Island and brought us here. Now your mom and I are going to let you sleep, but we'll be around if you need us."

All of a sudden, my mother starts crying hysterically and yells, "Look what they've done to my son!"

I write, *I will always need you.*

My father kisses me, and so does my mother. As they walk away, I think about this and realize that my father has never kissed me before, that I can remember.

CHAPTER 4

Straight Talk with the Doctor

AFTER MY PARENTS LEAVE, THE doctor returns and tells everyone else to leave so he can examine me. When they've all gone into the hallway, he closes the curtain around my bed. He looks at me with a fiery glare in his eye. "You've been doing entirely too much. After all, you've just woken up. I'll have to insist that you get more rest and have fewer visitors. If you continue, we'll have a serious fatigue issue here. The amount of blood you lost that we had to replace has made you very weak. I won't stand for this." Then his tone softens, and he smiles. "After all, I didn't spend six and a half hours putting you back together so that you could spoil all my excellent work. I'm sure you understand that the more rest you get, the better you'll start to feel and the quicker we can get you on your way home."

I write, *If I ask you some questions, will you give me straight answers?*

"I'll never lie to you, but do you mind if I examine you while we chat?"

I nod.

He begins to take my blood pressure.

I write, *Why can't I talk?*

He rolls up the blood pressure cuff, puts the stethoscope over his shoulders, and looks directly at me. "Well, young man, you do come right to the point, don't you? I could easily evade your question by telling you that the reason you can't speak is because we placed a tracheotomy tube in your throat. This tube is taking the air directly into your throat and into your lungs, rather than through your mouth or nose, so it prevents you from talking. That's one reason. But the real reason is because you had two lead pellets puncture your vocal chords."

I start to wonder what the hell I've been clobbered with. I write, *Will I ever be able to talk again?*

The doctor stops taking my pulse and looks at me. In his eyes, I see deep compassion, which warms me and scares me at the same time.

"I'm going to tell it to you straight. We think it's quite improbable that you'll be able to speak normally again. We did everything that we could possibly do. There were five surgeons, including the chief of surgery, working on you for over six and a half hours. Those men you ran into didn't leave us much to work with. By the time you were brought in here, you had already lost seven pints of blood and had swallowed quite a bit of your own blood and teeth."

This is all news to me. Up until now, I had no idea what had happened to me or how bad it really was. I run my partially numb tongue over my broken teeth. The pain is getting worse, but in spite of my pain and my fears, I have to find out the truth. I write, *Will I ever be able to breathe without the tubes and oxygen?*

"In this, I can give you a good answer. Yes, in time, depending on how fast you heal, we'll remove the tracheotomy tube from your throat and replace it with smaller ones. Eventually it will close itself. Then, hopefully, the tremendous damage that we repaired in your esophagus will mend, and you'll probably be able to breathe on your own."

Well, so far, I'm not doing too badly. All I keep hearing is *no*, *if*, and *maybe*. I write, *Will this damn pain ever go away?*

"You don't give a fellow a chance, do you?"

Not until you give me a better answer with a little hope instead of maybes and ifs.

"Well," he says, "to answer your question about the pain, it will subside in time. Next, I want to say that the hope I can give you is that you're more alive now than when I was first introduced to you two days ago. There was quite a bit of damage, and I think we did a good job, but only rest and time will give us the answers we need. No matter how this turns out, your life does not end here. You can still feel, move, see, and hear. Tomorrow, we'll get you up and see how you do. Your wife and family love you as much as they did before. More, I think. So do the hundreds of men in blue out there and even the nurses who've all been waiting around working double shifts, hoping you would open your eyes. You're strong. You can get better. You'll see."

I'm starting to get that choking feeling way down at the bottom of my throat. Of course the pain returns—the searing, stabbing pain that feels like dozens of steam-iron burns all over my face and throat.

Hope! It's such a simple word. It just rolls off the tip of your tongue.

The pain is getting worse. It's so bad that if I weren't strapped down, I would probably be running around pulling my hair out.

The doctor comes at me with the syringe. Once again, the pain subsides slowly, just enough to make me drowsy. The doctor pulls back the curtain from around the bed. He touches my arm and smiles as he walks away.

CHAPTER 5

Making Progress

S USAN WALKS UP TO MY bed and says, "You have a whole corridor full of friends out there who really want to see you so they can be convinced that you're alive."

I write, *I really don't know how to tell you this, but the doctor just gave me a shot for the pain and I feel really tired.*

"Okay, sweetheart, you sleep, and I'll tell the guys that you're not feeling well enough right now."

Thanks, honey. I'm sorry.

She smiles at me. "Don't be sorry. Right now, you're all that matters."

I watch her as she walks away, then start to drift off again. I really wish they would turn down the lights for just a while. It's so bright in here. *Please, God, don't let me dream again. Please, Lord, just a little sleep. Please!*

★ ★ ★

I become aware that I'm at the police academy, in a classroom taking an exam. I finish, and the whole class moves upstairs to the gym. We're getting instruction on takedown moves and how to handcuff subjects. There are about thirty-five probationary officers sitting on the mat area of the gym. The instructor asks for a volunteer, so I stand up.

"Well now, you're a bit light in your ass for what I wanted to show, but you'll do. Grab me from behind the neck."

The instructor is pretty tall, about six feet, ten inches, so I have to reach up to grab around his neck from behind.

Suddenly he steps to the left, pivots his feet, and throws me over his hip. I land on the mat, on my back, with enough force to register on the Richter scale. I break the impact of the fall by slapping the mat with my outstretched hand.

"Okay," he says. "Get up and try it again."

I get up and go around to his back and again reach up and grab his neck from behind. Again, he steps to the left, pivots his feet, and throws me to the mat. This action goes on two more times with no real instruction, just throwing me.

"Grab me again."

This time, I say to myself, it's going to be different.

I grab him. He steps to the left, pivots his feet for the throw, and I place my left hand in the small of his back, breaking the pivot and leverage he needs to throw me. I then slide my left foot under his legs and pull on his neck, and down he goes.

"Why?" he says.

"You're not teaching the throw and how to do it," I respond. "You're just throwing me over and over again. I didn't spend fifteen years studying karate and four years in the Marine Corps and do a tour in Vietnam just so you can treat me as a throwing

dummy. I don't mind being thrown, but at least teach them how it works."

He grabs my outstretched hand, and I help him up.

He pats me on the shoulder. "Good deal. I wasn't expecting that."

★ ★ ★

My senses are awakened by the dull metallic sound of the hospital PA system. The voice is requesting a doctor in room 1200. I look around the room and see that everything is the same. Nothing has changed. I must have just dozed off for a few minutes. I see Scotty standing in the hallway talking to a tall, heavy man. It occurs to me for the first time that Scotty is there not only as my friend, but also my protector. After all, I've been shot, and whoever shot me is still out there somewhere, maybe hoping to get rid of the star witness.

I try to think of a way to catch Scotty's attention. The pad and pen grab my eye, and I pick up the pen and tap it on the metal railing of my bed.

Scotty hears this and turns to see me. As he reaches the bed, he says, "How was your sleep?"

I feel a little better and stronger, but I only slept for a few minutes.

"A few minutes? You've been asleep for seventeen hours, since I left at four thirty yesterday afternoon."

I can't believe what he's saying. *What time is it?*

"It's nine thirty in the morning. Thursday."

Seventeen hours! It only felt like a few minutes. The cloud of sleep finally lifts from my head, and I realize I hadn't had a bad dream. The sleep was so refreshing because none of those stinking dreams invaded it.

A nurse arrives with my breakfast. She hands me a plastic cup with a white liquid in it. I place it to my lips and start to drink.

Her hand flies up and grabs my arm to stop me. "You can't drink that yet. From now on, you'll be getting this liquid every four hours. Because you have this tube in your throat that's an airway and goes directly into your lungs, we have to first inflate a tiny plastic inner tube that surrounds the base of the tracheotomy tube. This prevents the liquid from going into your lungs and drowning you. Now, to do that, we take this little plastic lead here and insert one end into the end of this needleless hypodermic. This will push air in and inflate the top of the tracheotomy tube. Once we do that, you have to drink quickly so we can then reverse the process so you can breathe. Got it?"

I nod, hoping I do.

"Here we go!" She pushes the plunger, and I can feel the tube enlarge in my throat. It's such a strange feeling that it makes my whole body shiver.

"There. Now you can drink. Quickly, all down at once."

I place the cup to my lips and swallow. As the cool liquid slides down what's left of my throat, I start to choke, but I finish it. I want to take a breath, but can't.

"Wait a second. Let me reverse this." She pulls back on the plunger.

I can feel the little tube deflate, and I can once again breathe. I write, *That stuff is disgusting. It tastes like ground-up chalk. What is it?*

"It's an antacid. Your stomach continues to produce

acids to break down your food, but since you're only getting your sustenance from the feeding tube, your stomach needs something to coat it."

You're kidding me! I have to keep drinking this crap?

"Yes, or you're sure to get an ulcer or worse."

After a little deliberation, I decide that I already have enough things wrong with me right now, so I'll continue to drink that nasty shit.

The Black doctor enters the room, followed by two other doctors, and they all stand around my bed.

I write, *I never asked your name.*

"I'm Dr. Obarto. Dr. Edwin Obarto."

"You have an accent I can't place. Are you from the West Indies?"

He laughs loudly. "I hope not. I'm from Nigeria, Africa."

I write, *How am I doing today?*

"Well, young man, let's take a look." He puts on plastic gloves and carefully starts to pull the bandages from my neck and throat and place them in a plastic bag. The adhesive on the bandages pulls my skin, and it hurts.

"I'm sorry for the discomfort of removing the bandages. It seems that these incisions are healing extremely fast. The swelling on your throat has gone down considerably, so I think we can do away with all these ice packs. You look a little stronger today. I understand you slept well?"

Yes! I write.

"Since you seem to be feeling stronger, we're going to get you up for a while today."

You mean I can walk around?

"Whoa! No, you can sit up in bed for a while. If you tried to stand up, you would become dizzy and pass out. It's going to take all your strength just to sit up." While he talks, he removes a pin from his white jacket. "Now, I'm going to stick you ever so gently with this pin in certain areas of your legs, throat, and neck, and I want you to raise your finger slightly if you feel it."

I watch intently as he makes a trail of jabs and sticks from my left upper thigh to the sole of my left foot. My hand practically stays in the air through the whole process. I get goose bumps on my arms every time I feel the pin pierce my skin, because that means that I have feeling in my leg. My goose bumps soon turn to shivers as I watch him stick the pin in my upper right thigh and I don't feel anything. No sensation at all. My heart drops. My mind is racing. Not only can't I talk or breathe on my own, now I'm going to be crippled.

The doctor sees the worried look on my face. "Now, you shouldn't get upset yet. There was some nerve damage on the right side of your neck and quite a bit of blunt trauma from the blast, which may explain the numbness in your right leg. These nerve endings will most probably heal, but then again, they may not. We'll have to try again tomorrow. In the meantime, I want to try your neck and throat area."

Although the tip of the pin finds its mark in my skin, somehow my brain is not notified of the sensation.

The doctor nods. "It's fine. I didn't expect any feeling in these areas yet. There was a lot of blunt trauma here. Now, young man, I'm going to ask one of your nurses to comb your hair and make you just a little more presentable to your family. Unfortunately, we can't shave you yet, but seeing you combed and sitting up will go a long way toward making your family feel a lot better, and it will make you feel better too."

Thank you, Doctor, I write.

"The only thanks you can give me, young man, is to rest, get strong, and leave this hospital on your own two feet instead of the way you were wheeled in here. No matter how popular you become, please remember this hospital."

Don't worry, Doctor. I could never forget what's been done for me here or the person who saved my life.

He smiles, touches my arm, and walks over to talk to the nurses.

CHAPTER 6

Mirror, Mirror

S COTTY COMES OVER TO THE bed. "How are you feeling, Bill?"

Sore as shit. Sometimes it burns, and other times it's like a hundred pins sticking in me. What was I shot with?

"You mean you don't know?" says Scotty.

I shake my head.

He pauses and takes off his hat. "You were hit with a twelve-gauge sawed-off shotgun loaded with number nine bird shot. You took four hundred pellets from thirteen feet away. Your bulletproof vest absorbed a hundred thirty-six pellets, so your life was saved by that stupid bulletproof vest we've always made fun of you for wearing."

I think back to when I first came on patrol. A salesman from a bulletproof vest company visited our precinct. He demonstrated how the vest fit and explained how it would stop bullets from penetrating our flesh. I was amazed. I knew I couldn't really afford the $125 it cost, but I knew I had to have it so I'd come home safe each night.

The nurses come over and ask Scotty to step out for a

second. As he leaves, they raise my bed, prop up my pillows, and start to comb my hair. Combing my hair is a job in itself. Dry blood matted to my hair crumbles off as they comb it.

While they slide my body up on the bed, I realize that the muscles in my neck can't support the weight of my head. I can't even help these people move me on the bed. I feel so damned helpless. I've never felt like this before.

The nurses are telling me how cute I look with my hair combed. I ask if I can have a mirror. A very nice brunette nurse hands me a small, round mirror, slightly smudged with fingerprints. I raise the mirror slowly to my face.

The image that stares back at me is someone I do not know, someone I've never seen before. I stare at where my cheeks and throat used to be. In their place, I see what seem like hundreds of little black holes. Instead of smooth pink flesh, there is raw, bruised, and discolored meat, torn, jagged, and hanging. I can't believe what I see. I think maybe I'm asleep and this is one of my nightmares. I was never really much to look at to begin with. I mean, it's not like I just stepped off the cover of *GQ* magazine, but now how am I going to walk around the rest of my life looking like this?

Suddenly, the fear and the hatred build up inside me. I pull my arm back and throw the mirror across the room. It smashes against the wall in a hundred pieces. This action pulls an IV line out of my arm.

The nurse who handed me the mirror runs to my side with tears in her eyes, as she realizes her mistake. "Don't go by what you see now in the mirror. Your face will clear up. You'll be fine."

You make sure I don't see anyone, I write. *No visitors at all. Not even my wife.*

"But Mr. Winder, listen to me . . ."

No one, I write. I throw the pad and pen to the floor.

As the nurse runs to the phone crying, I lie there starting to wonder how people are going to react in public when they see my face. I think back to my wedding day and how much trouble I went through just to look good, having my hair styled, shaving close while being very careful not to cut myself, and all the while thinking how I could never be physically attractive enough for my beautiful wife-to-be. I've always worried about my physical appearance. Now it seems the only thing I'll have to worry about is how to face people in public without them wincing and looking away in disgust.

As I lie there in serious thought about how I look, feeling sorry for myself, I notice a lumbering shadow over my bed. It's Dr. Obarto.

He pulls a chair up to the side of my bed and sits down. He places a brand-new pad and pen in my hand and looks at me sternly. "Since we've met, I've answered every question you've asked me truthfully, haven't I?"

Yes.

"Well, I'm telling you now that this mess you once recognized as your face will in a short time be back to the way you once knew it, save for a few hardly distinguishable scars."

Are you sure?

"When you were carried in here, there was a tremendous amount of damage. By the grace of God, we were afforded the time to do what was necessary to make you a whole person again. It's my profession to know how your skin is going to heal and how your body is going to react."

But I'm such a mess!

"You've been cut and scarred many times before, and you know that your body heals quickly. You're young and in good shape. You'll heal fast. All the holes you now see in your face are clean wounds and will disappear in time."

I'm sorry for giving the nurse a hard time, but when I saw my reflection, I was scared and angry.

"I realize how you must have felt, but don't punish the people who love and care about you and want to see you well again. The whole hospital staff has sort of adopted you, and they pray to see you well. You've become part of their family."

I nod, and we continue our discussion, with the doctor making me feel more relaxed about my situation and my looks. We talk for what seems to be hours, and I start to feel better. I hardly even notice the pain.

"Since you've seen fit to pull me away from the rest of my patients, I have an entirely new prescription for you," the doctor says. "First, you'll see your wife and the other members of your family who care about you. Then, you'll see the detectives waiting outside and give them an accurate account of what happened so they can catch these men. Then, if you aren't too tired, you'll see some of your fellow officers and convince them that you're feeling better so that when they go out on patrol, their minds will be on their job and nothing else."

I take the pen and start to write, but he stops me.

"Save your strength," he says. "You have a long day ahead of you, and tomorrow we have a surprise."

He walks away, and I can't help but notice the scent of the cologne he's wearing. It smells great. I remind myself to ask him what the name of it is.

After the doctor leaves, my wife enters with my brothers-in-law, Harold and Lenny. They are still dressed in their work clothes and look terribly tired. It's good to see them. They tell me how much all my nieces and nephews miss me and are praying for me. They sit and talk to me for a while and then they leave so my sisters-in-law, Toni and Debra, can see me. We talk, and they fluff my pillows and fuss over me. After a while, my other brother-in-law, Phil, and his wife, Mary, come in. They tell me that my wife will be fine staying with them for a while until I come home. I want so much to be able to talk to these two who, since I've met them, have treated me with love and kindness, but I guess they'll have to get used to me writing things down.

We visit for a while, and then two men in suits walk up to the bed and tell me they're detectives. They're hoping that I can give them an accounting of what happened, since I'm the only witness that they know about to my own attempted murder.

I pick up the pen and pad and write, *The only way I can communicate is by writing it down. I'm sorry.*

"Listen, Officer, don't apologize. Any light you can shed on this will be helpful. If you get tired, let us know and we can come back later."

I explain to them that as I write, it will mostly be abbreviated, because it would take too much writing to get through it all, and I get tired fast. They explain that they understand.

I prop the pad up on my knees and begin to write.

> *I was on my normal routine patrol at the 176th and Jerome Avenue Station on the elevated line, when I was approached by an unidentified Black male who said that he thought there may be a robbery taking place downstairs in the bar because as he walked by he saw everyone in the bar with their hands up. I thanked him and went to the token booth and told the clerk to call on the system phone to the district office and request a 10-13, officer in danger, and also tell them there was a robbery in progress. I then proceeded to the station window that overlooks the bar. As I looked out the window at the front door of the bar, I noticed there was a light-blue car with out-of-state license plates parked about three feet from the curb.*
>
> *At this point, I took out my handheld radio and spoke into the box. "Eleven assignment 74 requesting a 10-13 at 176th Street and Jerome Avenue, in the street. Possible robbery in progress. Acknowledge!"*
>
> *There was dead silence. I started down the stairs leading to the street very slowly, constantly watching the bar door in case they*

came out and all the time listening for the music in the bar, knowing that if the music gets louder, that means someone opened the bar door.

As I descended halfway down the stairs, I tried my radio again. "Eleven assignment 74, requesting a 10-13 at 176ᵗʰ Street and Jerome Avenue, in the street. Possible robbery in progress. Acknowledge!"

Still, there was no sound. No response from this little gray box that was supposed to be our vital link with the department in case of emergency.

I cursed the radio for never working in the six years that I had tried to use it on this line and placed it back in its holder on my belt. I decided that if I didn't take some action, innocent people might be hurt. Realizing no one heard my radio call for help, I started to descend down the rest of the stairs to the street.

I draw a makeshift diagram for the detectives so they can plot each of my movements and location.

While I write on the pad, I'm trying to be very accurate, but it's difficult because I'm forced to write a lot. I can't shorten the writing even though it's an exhausting task, for fear of giving a wrong detail. *Excuse me*, I write. *I'm suddenly exhausted. Can I stop for a while?*

"Of course. We'll come back later. You rest."

My eyelids are so heavy, I can't keep them open.

CHAPTER 7

Getting Better, but Will the Dreams Ever Stop?

I'M SITTING IN THE LUNCHEONETTE *across from the police academy with my friend Johnny.*

Johnny is a bit overweight but a really nice guy.

"Bill," he says, "I'm terrible at the physical stuff in our training. I need to lose weight or I'm never going to pass the physical endurance test at the end of our class. You're great at the physical stuff. You're having a problem with the academics and need a bit of help there. If I help tutor you in criminal procedure law, penal law, and other academics, will you help show me how to lose weight and pass the endurance test?"

"That's a deal," I say.

We push our food away and start opening our books.

Time speeds by as I help him with sit-ups, push-ups, his diet, and running. He helps explain the different statutes of the law and how they apply. I teach him how to disarm and subdue a felon. He teaches me about issuing tickets, about criminal procedure law, penal law, and how to fill out reports. We work well, and a strong bond of friendship is created.

Six months go by very quickly. We've been given instruction on deadly physical force and are allowed to carry our loaded weapons. We're at the last day of testing. I score an 86 on my finals in the academics. Johnny scores a 75 in the physical. He's lost 25 pounds. He's able to jump onto the train tracks, pick up and lift a 125-pound dummy, place it on the platform, and then jump onto the platform himself.

"That's great!" I say. "We passed."

Johnny is so happy. We hug each other and get dressed for the ride home.

We're at the graduation ceremony, where we get to shake hands with the chief of police and the police commissioner.

★ ★ ★

My eyes open, and I'm back at the intensive care ward. I look up and tell the officer guarding me to call the detectives back.

They come to my bedside, and I write, *Let's get this done.*

The detectives remind me of where we left off, and I finish telling them about what happened. They thank me and leave.

I look up at the doorway of the ICU and see a team of four people in white coats coming toward my bed. Among them is Dr. Obarto. He winks at me.

The doctor in the front says, "We're going to look inside your mouth into your throat. I want to see how much damage was done."

I nod.

He puts a strap with a round, shiny mirror on his forehead and leans in real close. "Say ahhhhhhh."

I open my mouth as wide as I can. He puts a tongue

depressor on my tongue and starts to put a long mirror down the back of my throat.

I choke and gag.

"Try and hold still and not move."

I don't know how many people have found themselves in this actual scenario, but believe me, it's very scary and awkward.

I open my mouth again, and he again puts the depressor on my tongue and looks in my throat with the mirror.

Again, I gag and shake my head.

"Here," he says. "One of you hold his tongue with this gauze pad."

I open wide, and another doctor takes my tongue with the gauze pad and holds it. The first doctor puts the mirror down my throat and points a flashlight into my throat. He looks around for a few seconds and then the other doctor lets go of my tongue. The one with the mirror and flashlight steps back and talks to the other doctors so low I can't hear.

As they walk away, taking off their gloves, I write, *Who is he and what just happened?*

"He's the leading speech specialist in the city," says Dr. Obarto, who has stayed behind. "He says you have too much swelling right now for him to form an opinion. That's why you can't make any sounds. We'll try again tomorrow. In the meantime, we'll place the ice packs on you again for tonight to try and bring down the swelling. Sleep well, and I'll see you tomorrow."

My throat is so sore from the probing that it needs to be cleaned out again. I start to settle in, and the nurses come over and put the ice packs on my neck. I feel like I'm in a freezer.

The nurses wheel in another bed and fill the empty space on my left. The patient in the bed is a Black guy with a huge bandage on his stomach. After they have him situated, they leave, and we're alone.

"Hey!" he says to me as he tries to lift himself off of the bed. "Hey, you're that guy! You're that cop I saw on TV. You got shot in the face. You're getting pretty famous."

I write on the pad and hold it so he can see it. *What happened to you?*

"I guess I pushed my old lady a bit too far. She wanted me to go to church, but I refused to go. I wanted to watch the game, you know? So she picked up a knife and cut me."

His name is Richard. We talk for quite a while, sharing stories about our jobs and his kids. I have to write large letters because he's a little distance away. Without warning, the lights get turned off so we can actually get some sleep. I wave to him. I hear him praying out loud.

When he's finished, he looks at me. "I said a prayer for you. I hope you get better fast. What they did to you was wrong."

I think to myself, *I hope I get better too.*

Sleep comes slowly. It's been a very long day.

★ ★ ★

I find myself with my squad in the Que Son Valley in Vietnam. We discover a hole in the ground. I know it's a tunnel entrance. I start shucking off my outer equipment and rifle. The sergeant hands me a flashlight and a .45-caliber automatic pistol.

I refuse these and remove my knife from its scabbard. I turn and enter the hole. I slide down to the bottom, about ten feet.

I get to my knees and start crawling forward. I crawl about fifteen feet and come to a sharp left bend in the tunnel. I smell a lit cigarette. I wait there on my knees. I'm not worried about being detected, because I've learned to eat Vietnamese food. Your body odor becomes permeated with what you eat, so when I sweat, I smell like a Vietnamese.

The VC snuffs out his cigarette on the side of the wall and starts crawling in my direction. As he reaches the sharp turn, he lifts his left hand up to grab the wall for balance, and it's over that quick. One second. One second changes his entire world. One second in time, and I've taken away everything he had, and anything he ever would have had.

I continue to the short end of the tunnel. I find food, the makings for booby traps, and ammo for an AK-47.

★ ★ ★

My head starts to spin, and I awake instantly, choking and sputtering. The nurses run over and clean my tube. Man, I hate that shit. I manage a weak smile, and one of them squeezes my shoulder as they adjust my sheets and ice packs.

I wonder if the dreams will ever leave me alone, if they will ever stop haunting me.

It's still dark out and I'm exhausted, but I'm afraid to go to sleep. Instead, I lie there thinking of all kinds of bad crap. *What's going to happen to me?*

I lie there for what seems like forever. I watch out the window. Dawn is coming, and soon light makes its way through the window blinds and lights up the whole room.

The fellow next to me asks, "Not much sleep, huh?"

I shake my head.

"Your face looks thinner today. I think your swelling has gone down a lot."

The hospital's morning rounds start. Blood tests for patients, temperatures, medications, and blood pressure. Then they roll in a cart, and I can smell the food. I'm very anxious. The nurse comes over and takes a hypodermic needle and pushes air into the trach tube to inflate the little round tube in my throat that allows me to swallow and not choke. She hands me the little cup with that nasty liquid I have to drink a few times a day to counteract the acids my stomach creates to digest the food.

I swallow it down, and she fills the tube back up so I can breathe. She checks my IV bottles, straightens out my sheets, smiles, and walks away. She comes back with a small cart with a white bowl and clothes and towels. She starts to give me a bath while I'm in the bed. Now this may sound nice, but it's very embarrassing and makes me feel chilled.

Dr. Obarto comes into the room. He smiles and says, "Good morning." He checks my eyes, my tubes, and my neck. "The swelling has gone down considerably. How do you feel this morning? I understand you were up most of the night."

I write, *I'm okay.*

"We're going to try an experiment today. We're going to see if we can't get you to sit in this chair by your bed here for a while. How does that sound?"

Great.

He can see I'm very excited. He calls the nurse over.

The doctor requests a tray, and they pull my covers off, exposing my genital area, which they cover with a blue paper sheet. The doctor takes hold of the catheter tube. I get nervous and start to fidget.

He says, "Oh, I forgot to mention, we're removing your catheter tube today."

Let me tell you something. I was unconscious when they inserted this tube, so I don't know how much it hurt when it went in. I do, however, know how much it hurt coming out.

When this process is complete and the tube is taken away, two nurses come over and each holds my arms while the doctor slides my feet and legs over the side of the bed. Moving like this hurts a lot. Moving makes all my incisions move and hurt. I start to get dizzy. My head flops around because the muscles in my neck aren't supporting my head weight.

"Take a minute," the doctor says. "Let your body adjust to sitting up."

I nod.

They all lift me up until my feet are touching the floor. Again, I feel dizzy, and again, we stop for a moment. I start to fall backward, and they all tighten their grip on my arms. A brief minute goes by, and I nod.

Again, they hold me and turn me so the chair is right behind me. They lower me down into the chair.

"Careful," the doctor says. "Don't let him go down too fast."

With great difficulty, I sit. They get sheets and blankets to put around me and two pillows to prop my head. They adjust my IV stands so that they're on either side of me. I must have looked a sight sitting there all bundled up with IV bottles attached to me on both sides.

"There," the doctor says. "How is that?"

I nod.

"We'll only try this for a little while. It will tire you at first and you'll be dizzy, but we need to get you moving a little, and I think sitting up like this will make you feel better about yourself."

I nod, and they all slip away.

Bill Winder, Que Son Mountains, Vietnam 1968

Getting ready for the midnight tour

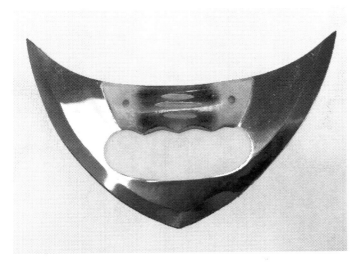

The knife I used in Vietnam as a tunnel rat.
I had it specially made in Da Nang.

Being inducted into the Martial Arts Hall of Fame

Being awarded the New York City Transit
Police Department Medal of Honor

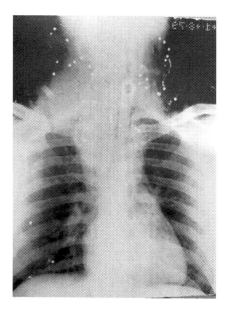

X-ray of my face, throat, and upper chest after being hit with the shotgun blast. Notice the remaining pellets. On the bottom left are two pieces of teeth I swallowed. Right in the center at the top of my throat area, you can see the tracheotomy tube.

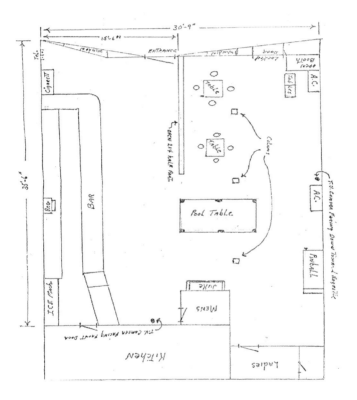

Drawing of the inside of the bar that I
did months after the shooting

CHAPTER 8

Okay, I'm Here; What Do I Do Now?

SCOTTY COMES TOWARD ME AND gets very happy when he sees me. He smiles and says, "Look at you, all sitting up and everything."

I search for my pad and pen, and Scotty grabs it off the bed and hands it to me.

I write, *It feels strange, and I'm dizzy.*

"It's okay," he says. "You'll be fine. You're strong."

One of the nurses pushes a rolling side table over and places it in front of me. "Here's a little desk for you." She takes a comb from her pocket and combs my hair. "Now you'll look presentable to everyone."

My wife comes in. "Hey, look at you all sitting up. How are you feeling?"

Not bad, just tired and dizzy. It's really good to see you.

She kisses me and steps back. "I brought your parents with me. Wait till they see you sitting up!"

My mother and father come in, and as soon as they see me, my mother puts her hands to her face. They both look happy.

My father grabs my hand. "You look good sitting there, boy. You look tired though, and your color is off. How are they feeding you?"

A nurse comes up. "Funny you should mention that." She holds up a little white paper cup and the empty hypo. "It's lunchtime. I think you all need to step out for just a minute."

Everyone steps out, and we go through the process of deflating my tube and me drinking the liquid chalk, then being put back to the way I was. The nurse cleans everything up, checks my tube and IVs, and walks away. Everybody comes back in.

"How often do they do that?" my mother asks. "I saw through the curtain."

I write, *So far, about six times a day. Although I can't breathe through my mouth, I still have working taste buds. And it's awful.*

"I'll bet. Is that going to be a permanent thing?"

I write, *I don't know yet.*

At that moment, the doctors from the day before arrive. The same specialist steps up to the bed and asks everyone to leave. He smiles at me and says, "Say aahhhhh!"

I open my mouth, but of course, nothing comes out. He grabs my tongue with gauze again and looks down my throat. He moves his head and the flashlight back and forth, and tells me to swallow.

I do, but it hurts.

He let's go of my tongue. "I'm going to cover the tube. I want you to say 'hi.'"

I nod, and he places a gauze pad over the tube. I try to

say "hi," and I feel a little air in the top of my throat, but nothing comes out.

"Again," he says. "Concentrate!"

I try again, and this time I can hear a faint "hi."

He takes away the gauze pad and smiles. "The swelling is down a lot. There doesn't seem to be any infection, but we'll continue the antibiotics for a while longer. Continue with the tube and feedings. It looks very promising." He looks down at me. "Though we aren't home yet, that should make you feel a little better. We know the potential and ability are there. We need to see how much comes back the stronger you get. I'm pleased. I'll see you again in two days."

As the specialist turns and they walk away, Dr. Obarto squeezes my hand. I can see my wife and parents in the hall talking to the doctors, and they look very relieved. They come back in and gather around my bed. We're all pretty happy. My wife tells me about what's going on in the press and at home with my nephews and nieces, and the time passes.

A nurse comes over after about four hours and takes my blood pressure and my temperature. "Both are high," she says. "I think that's enough for today. We need to let him rest and build up his strength."

We all say good-night, and Scotty stays behind to say his good-night.

I write, *Can I have a newspaper or a TV?*

"No, I'm sorry you can't yet. They don't want you to see anything in the news or press that might contaminate your ID of the culprits. Tomorrow, if they let you sit up again, we can play some cards."

I grew up watching a lot of television, so I really miss it. We nod to each other, and he goes back out in the hall to his post. Dinnertime comes and then the job of getting me back into bed, which seems to be a lot more work than getting me out. The nurse comes with a pain shot, and I shake my head.

"Are you sure?"

I nod, and she says okay and walks away.

I'm so very tired. I know I'll sleep tonight. My eyelids start to close, and I'm out.

CHAPTER 9

Can I Have a Little Privacy?

I'M STANDING IN THE STREET *by a subway staircase. I have one culprit on the ground, and I see two more under the staircase, kneeling down. I spin around with my service revolver, and out of the corner of my right eye, I see a figure and I try to move my feet. They feel like they're cemented down. I can't move. I know what's going to happen, but I can't do anything to stop it.*

Then it happens. The flash and the dozens of burnings in my throat and face, and I'm forced awake abruptly, coughing and sputtering, grabbing at the air.

★ ★ ★

The nurse runs over, calms me down, and reminds me where I am. "You need to take this pain medication," she insists. "This is no time to try and tackle all these issues at once. You need rest."

I nod, and she injects me. A few minutes later, the searing, stabbing pain subsides, and I slip off.

★ ★ ★

Each day in the hospital pretty much goes the same. I sleep, I dream, I wake up trying to scream, they clean out my throat, I see my family, I drink chalk, and I sleep and dream.

By the fifth day, I'm sitting in the chair next to my bed, and Scotty and I are playing cards. The group of doctors comes in, and one asks Scotty to step out for a minute. The specialist leans down, takes a gauze pad, and holds my tongue. He looks down my throat with the flashlight. He lets my tongue go and stands up straight. He places another piece of gauze over my trach hole. "Say 'hi.'"

I swallow and say very slowly, "Hi there, Doc."

He smiles and takes the gauze away. "Very nice. There's no infection, so we can stop the antibiotic. I think his speech will be fine. I want to give him a barium exam, just as a precaution, to rule out any holes that may have been overlooked during the surgery. Remove the tube in his throat and replace it with the next smaller size down. This way, it'll start to close, and we can get him breathing normally again. Also, remove the feeding tube from his nasal area. We can try him on real food soon." As he walks away, he shoots me a thumbs-up.

Dr. Obarto tells the nurse, "We can remove the IV with the antibiotic, and also the tube as directed." He turns to me. "Very nice, Bill, you'll be out of here in no time."

He leaves, and the nurses remove one IV, replace my tube with a smaller one, and change my bandages. They then proceed to remove the tube that's down my nose and providing nourishment to my stomach. It's an incredibly strange feeling indeed. I feel very tired, so they leave the room.

I have an extremely strong urge to go to the bathroom. I find it embarrassing to sit on a metal bowl, so I decide to get up and go to the bathroom by myself. I push the blanket off of me and reach up and grab the IV pole and pull myself up. I take a second to catch my balance, and I start to walk forward. As I walk, I glide the IV pole with me, using it as a cane.

I slide right past everyone, and no one notices. Down the hall, four doors on the right, is a staff bathroom. I step inside, shut the door, and sit down. I feel bad that I'm doing this sneaky thing and not telling anyone, but I let out a sigh of relief that I'm sitting comfortably with some privacy, finally. I can't begin to tell you what a simple, free, undisturbed moment like this feels like. It's a true blessing to be able to find privacy for this much-needed private moment.

Everything is going well until all of a sudden, I hear over the hospital PA system, "Officer Winder, please report back to ICU. Officer Winder, please report back to ICU."

I hear people running up and down the hallway, and I feel like a little kid in trouble. When I'm done, I open the door slightly. In the hall staring at me are two nurses, two officers, and Dr. Obarto. He glares at me with burning eyes.

I look up sheepishly and slide out into the hallway.

Dr. Obarto says, "Slowly and carefully, walk him back to his bed. Prepare him for moving to a regular room so he can have some privacy. Remove the other IV and remove the throat tube and switch it to the smallest size." He looks at me. "This is not a reward. I just think it's time."

We get back to my bed, and they lay me down. Scotty and I are laughing.

"This isn't funny, you know," a nurse says. "You scared the crap out of all of us."

I place my hand to my heart as if to say I'm sorry. I'm wheeled to an elevator, and we ride up to the fourth floor. They wheel me into a private room all the way at the end of the wing, position my bed, and fix my pillows.

I write, *Can I have a TV now?*

"No, I'm afraid not," Scotty says. "Not yet, but soon I hope."

I nod that I understand.

I'm really exhausted, and my eyes close as I try to fight sleep. When I sleep, I dream, and the dreams are never good.

I really don't want to sleep. I'd rather think of some funny stuff that's happened to me, so I can try and get away from thinking about all the bad stuff. I start to think, and immediately, my mind goes to one night when I was working a midnight shift. I stopped to patrol one of my stations, 116th Street and Lenox Avenue on the IND line. It was about 2:00 a.m. I was talking to the token booth clerk, when out of the corner of my right eye, I saw a figure running down the stairs. He ran past me, completely naked except for a T-shirt. He went through the gate at the turnstiles without paying a fare. I started to go after him, and a female, also completely naked, came running down the stairs. She also went through the gate onto the platform. I couldn't believe what I was seeing. It was February 12 and about twenty degrees outside. I walked through the gate and started heading toward them.

A big man about six feet, two inches tall, fully clothed, came through the gate looking really pissed off. He ran past me, grabbed the naked guy, and started hitting him. The woman screamed. I ran up and ordered the clothed guy to stop hitting the naked man. He ignored me.

Now, I spent four years in the Marine Corps, and I had been teaching karate classes for a long time, so my voice could get real loud. I yelled at him again to stop hitting the man, and I raised my nightstick over my shoulder in a striking position. He looked at me, stopped, and stepped back. I told them all to calm down and talked to them for ten minutes, trying to figure out what was going on.

It turned out the clothed man was at work as a truck driver. His run ended early, and he came home and surprised his wife in bed with what turned out to be his best friend. They talked it over, and no one wanted to press charges. They all walked away, talking, and went back up the stairs to the street.

As I remember this, I think to myself, *New York City. You can't make this shit up.*

CHAPTER 10

Finally, a Shower

M Y EYES OPEN, AND I feel with my tongue along the inside of my mouth, gliding over the rough, jagged surface of broken teeth. I look up, and my parents are staring down at me.

My father says, "Listen, Willie boy, we're so glad you're feeling so much better and they've moved you into this private room. Your doctor says you're healing very quickly, and he wouldn't be surprised if you were going home in a couple of days. Your mom and I hate to leave, but we need to get back to Rhode Island to take care of your niece and nephew. We love you, and we'll call every day to see how you are."

I nod and kiss my mom as she leans in to give me a hug.

When they leave, Dr. Obarto comes in with a new officer there to guard me, who introduces himself as John Simons.

The doctor examines me and says I'm healing really fast and that the throat specialist will be in to see me early tomorrow morning. In the meantime, before I have any visitors, he has a surprise. I'm to take a shower. He slowly removes my bandages and takes a look. He touches a few spots with his gloved finger and nods that I'm ready.

I'm excited to be getting a shower. It's been many days that I've lain in dried blood. Even though I've had sponge baths, they're not the same as the real thing.

"Take your time walking," Dr. Obarto tells me. "The shower is two doors down on your right. The nurses have already put fresh soap, shampoo, and three towels in there for you, along with fresh underwear and fresh pajamas your wife brought for you. You have no more IVs, so you won't be limited in getting your clothes on. Take your time. I'm serious. And above all else, cover the hole of the tube. Don't let water get in there."

I nod as I slide my feet and legs over the side of the bed. I stand up carefully, and Officer Simons grabs my right arm. We slowly walk down the hall to the shower room. He helps me into the shower and then steps outside. I take off my hospital gown and drop it outside the stall. I turn the water on, and the warm water pelts my face and body. It feels so good. All of a sudden, I feel a rush of dizziness, and I start to fall backward. I'm so scared. I can't stop myself.

The room spins, and I start to fall. I feel a strong hand reach in and grab my arm. It holds me upright.

Officer Simons slides the shower curtain a little to the side and looks at me. "I'm sorry to intrude," he says, "but you didn't look good and I thought you might need help."

I'm very embarrassed but thankful he's there. He holds my arm as I wash myself and shampoo my hair. As I wash, I think that this small amount of help Simons is affording me is the true meaning of one officer having the other officer's back, no matter what. I know he'll never tell anyone this, and I've never mentioned it until now. It still humbles me to think about it.

I'm careful not to let water or soap get into my tracheotomy. The warm rivulets cascading off my face and body quickly turn dark-reddish-brown. I watch it as the liquid circles down the drain, dried bits of caked-on blood dripping off of me and intermingling with the suds and water.

Finally, I'm done. Officer Simons hands me a towel and asks how I feel. I look at him and nod. He hands me another towel and steps outside of the shower room.

I carefully dry myself and step sideways to the mirror. A slightly swollen face looks back, with many small black pockmarks on my lower face and throat. I stare at the tracheotomy tube sticking out of my throat and reach out and almost touch the long lines of stitched skin on either side of my throat. *Don't think about that, Bill*, I say to myself. *It'll get better.*

I dry off and slide into new underwear and pajamas. I comb my hair but decide not to try to shave myself yet. I have enough scars now without messing with a razor and causing more.

I start to clean up my dirty clothes and used towels, but a nurse comes in and says, "Don't be silly. We'll clean that up. You need to get back to bed now."

She takes my arm, and we slowly walk out of the shower room. As we step out, Officer Simons grabs my other arm, and we walk down the hall to my room. It's amazing how a simple task like a shower can tire you out so quickly. As we step inside, my wife and two brothers-in-law, Harold and Lennie, are waiting for me.

Harold says, "He doesn't look bad at all." He helps me back into bed. "The kids miss you very much. They knew they couldn't come to see you, so they made an audiotape for you."

He turns on the tape player, and I sit there listening to his five kids tell me they love and miss me.

I look around my new hospital room. I have a window that faces the street, very nice. I lie down in my new bed and listen to all the updates of my nieces and nephews and how things are going at home. My wife comes in and tells me that my sister, Jane, is here and wants to see me. She informs me that Jane has come every day. My sister is three years older than me and ran away from our home at sixteen years old. She fell in love with an older guy and was introduced to drugs and prostitution soon after. She's been the cause of countless sleepless nights for my parents, who for many years chased her around to try and rescue her over and over again.

I look at my wife, remembering all the pain and drama my sister usually causes, and I write, *I don't want to see her. Don't let her in.*

"Are you sure?"

I write, *Under no circumstances is she to be let in here. I know it's hard for you to say that to her, but that's what I want.*

"Okay, honey."

After she leaves, I lie there and start to reminisce about some of my sister's exploits. One day, she said she was going out to buy a pack of cigarettes and didn't come back for six months. Remembering these times just strengthens the feeling I have of how much I hate my sister. I feel sleep coming on, but I'm apprehensive because sleep means dreaming, and the dreams are never good.

As my eyes close, my wife returns. She notices how I'm falling asleep and leans in and kisses my forehead. She sits on the bed next to me. My last thoughts are of my sister. I think of how she can get into your heart and then steal a hot stove.

★ ★ ★

I'm walking down a staircase in an underground subway station. It's a staircase that people use to get from the subway to the bus outside. I patrol the staircase because I know there are youths who hide in the staircase to rip people off. As I get to the bottom of the first landing and turn the corner, I'm suddenly grabbed and thrown down the next flight of stairs. When I get to the bottom and look back up, there's no one there.

I'm extremely pissed off as I pick myself up and brush off my uniform. I'm not badly injured, just more embarrassed than anything else. I really want to keep this to myself, but I know I have to write a report about it. As I board the next train leaving the station to go back to the district house, I notice that everyone in the subway car is very nervous. I look around, and I see a young Black man about twenty years old, cleaning his fingernails with a nice six-inch folding knife.

I slowly walk over to him and look down at him. "Hi, how're you doing? Nice knife."

He looks up. "Yeah."

"Do you see all these people in this car?"

"Yeah."

"They're kind of nervous because you're picking your nails

with that knife. That makes them scared. In the law, it's called intimidation."

"So?"

"So, I need you to put that away."

He stands up and faces me, and the hand with the knife drops down to his side.

Now, I'm still sore and annoyed from being thrown down a flight of stairs, so I say, "Listen, all you have to do is put it away. You sit down, and I walk away. It's that simple."

As we're standing there face-to-face, my nightstick is resting on my shoulder. I look into his face and see a twitch of thought in his eye. He tries to bring the knife up from the right side while he's watching the nightstick on my shoulder. With his attention distracted, I hit his wrist with my fist. He screams in pain and drops the knife. I bend over, pick up the knife, and turn him around and start to place handcuffs on his wrists. As I lead him off the subway car at the next stop to call for a car, a crowd is waiting to board the train.

He starts screaming, "Help me! Somebody help me! This white cop is beating me up. I didn't do anything."

The crowd hesitates and starts to face me. One big fellow says, "Why don't you let the brother go?"

I look at him. I pull out the knife, open it up, and hold it in his face. "He had this knife," I said, "and he was using it in a threatening manner. I told him to put it away, and he attacked me with it. Now, you may feel sympathy for him, but the truth is, he would stab you or your mother or anyone else. It's my job to stop him. It's what you pay me to do. And that is exactly what I intend to do." I look around. "Anyone else?"

The crowd turns and gets into the subway car. A huge man from the train walks up to me. "Officer, I'll wait here with you until your ride comes just to help."

"Thank you, sir."

"No, thank you *for protecting us."*

★ ★ ★

As my eyes open, I see that the sun is shining into my room window. It's morning.

Dr. Obarto is there by the bed, looking at my throat. "First, we're removing the final tube today and allowing the small hole in your throat to close on its own. Second, we're going to get you some real food and stop the antacid. This should help in making you stronger faster." He sees that I'm smiling. "Now before we can give you food, I need to send you for an upper GI series to make sure there are no holes we missed."

I write, *How does that work?*

"You drink this liquid, and we take a picture as the liquid goes through your esophagus."

Sounds like fun.

He says, "The liquid taste like the antacid you've been drinking."

Great, I write.

CHAPTER 11

Okay, so I'm Not Superman

D OWN IN THE X-RAY ROOM, they give me this large plastic cup with the disgusting white crap in it. They place me in front of the x-ray machine's screen and tell me to drink the mixture slowly so that they can watch how it goes down my throat, to see if there are any perforations that they missed. There are none, thank God.

I come back from the test and find that everything is okay. I also find my lunch sitting there waiting for me. I start to open the food tray and find a boiled chicken leg.

The nurse grabs me. "Not yet. First we remove the last tube."

We go into the bathroom, and I lean over the sink. She reaches up, removes the tape surrounding the tube, and removes the tube from the inside of my throat. If you've never had a breathing tube in your throat and then had it removed, I guarantee you, it's a feeling I wouldn't wish on anyone.

She covers the hole with gauze and tape. "Now you can eat, but slowly. Your throat may still be raw."

I sit down, pick up the chicken, and bite into it. I immediately taste the most pleasant and delicious chicken I've ever had in my life. I'm sure it's because I haven't eaten for days. After all, it's just boiled chicken, with no seasoning. After my second bite, I realize two things. The nurse was right about my throat still being raw. The food burns on the way down. But I also notice that I really don't have a lot of teeth to bite with. I know that's why I'm having boiled chicken. It doesn't require hard chewing.

As I'm trying to eat, my wife walks in. "Wouldn't a fork make that easier?"

I suddenly realize that I've been using my hands to eat. I was so hungry, I hadn't noticed. I grab the napkin and wipe my face. I take a sip of my milk, cold as it goes down my throat. It feels good. I fix my coffee with sugar and milk, and as I bring it to my lips, I remember back at the district, lining up for noon-to-8:00 p.m. roll call. We had a sergeant—I won't mention his name—who brought a big cup of coffee to the roll call podium every tour. As he read our assignments and responsibilities, he would sip the coffee. Now being the joker that I am, I took out my partial upper dental bridge—I lost my four front teeth to a round kick at a tournament when I was seventeen—and placed them in his coffee when he was in the other room.

As he read the roll call, he sipped the coffee. By the time he was done talking to us and ready to dismiss us, he took the last sip and saw my teeth in the bottom of the cup. "Winder, you asshole!" he screamed.

Everyone laughed hard and pointed at him. It was funny, but it cost me two days' suspension without pay.

Back to the present. My wife says, "I'm so glad to see

you're finally eating. Wow, look, your tube is gone. You're almost human again."

I look up at her and continue to eat.

Just then, the same two detectives who came before walk in carrying a book. "Sorry to disturb your meal, but do you think you can look at some pictures for us?"

I write, *Yes.*

They place the big book on my lap and open it. "Now, you just keep turning the pages and looking at the pictures until you see someone who looks familiar."

I start to turn the pages and come on the first one I recognize. I point to the picture.

"Are you sure?"

I nod.

"Which one was he?"

The driver. I continue flipping through the book of pictures and stop and point to another picture.

"Which was he?"

Under the stairs. I continue picking out each culprit until I come to a picture and stare at it for a long time. I can't take my eyes off it. I start to shake.

"Is he one?"

I don't answer him but continue to look at the picture.

The detective takes my hand.

I look up at him.

"Is he one?"

I nod.

"Which one?"

I look at him and write, *SHOTGUN!*

He says, "Good. Good. You picked out all four guys. Great job."

I look down at the floor.

"What?" he asks.

If I had done a good job, I'd have collared them all and not got shot.

He drops the book and looks at me. He finally says, "Who are you? Superman? Do you have a big red *S* on your chest? Do you break dates with Lois Lane? *No!* You had three culprits down and were covering them. You didn't see the fourth guy in the back seat of the car. And you got clobbered. Do you think any two or three cops could have done better? You pointed them out. We'll get them. You protected those people in that bar. You had the vision and forethought to buy your own bulletproof vest. None of us did that. You survived. Don't blame yourself. You didn't shoot yourself. They did."

I nodded.

The detectives say thanks and leave.

A voice from the doorway says, "They're right, you know." The man with the voice comes into the room. It's my old captain. He sits down in a chair across from me. "None of us ever know it's going to turn out like this. We just suit up and do the job. I saw your family history when you first came under me. I knew your military record and what your values were. I knew you would make a good cop. With this incident, you've opened a lot of eyes. You're going to be in the spotlight for a while. I'm proud of you. If you need anything, just call me."

I write, *Thanks, Captain.*

He gets up slowly, pats me on the shoulder, and leaves the room.

Seeing the captain reminds me of when he came to me

one day and told me that a new sergeant was coming into the district. He told me he was a hard-ass, and he would certainly not put up with any of my jokes.

When the sergeant reported in, he brought his clothes and put them in his locker. He closed the locker door and went back upstairs to get another load. I went upstairs too. I looked around. It was pouring rain. I saw this stray dog walking around in the rain and mud. He was soaked and filthy. I got an idea and put my nightstick tong loop around his neck and guided him downstairs to the district. No one said a word, and I brought the dog into the sergeant's locker room. I opened the new sergeant's locker door, looked inside at all the freshly cleaned uniforms, and stuck the dog in his locker.

The sergeant came in carrying more uniforms and went to his locker and opened it. Out jumped a big muddy, filthy dog, shaking his fur violently and getting all the uniforms filthy.

Everyone laughed. I got three days' suspension for that one.

★ ★ ★

The day nurse comes in and fixes my bed linen. I use this opportunity to slip into my private bathroom for some alone time. What a feeling to be able to navigate around without the cumbersome IV lines and stands and the tube in my throat.

Dr. Obarto arrives a little later. He just stands there and looks at me. With a smile, he says, "Good afternoon."

I start to write an answer on my pad.

Before I can, he grabs my hand, looks at me, and says,

"Good afternoon." He points at my mouth and places a finger on the gauze covering the hole in my throat.

It comes out scratchy and slightly hoarse when I say, "Good afternoon."

He takes his finger away, and my eyes start to fill up. "If you must cry, go ahead," he says. "There's nothing to stop you."

I feel so relieved, like a huge weight has just been removed from my chest. I cover the gauze and thank him. "I can't tell you how happy I am right now."

"Thank God! I just moved the scalpel. He guided my hand and sat on your shoulder and decided your work on this Earth wasn't done yet."

"I thank God and you and everyone in this hospital," I reply.

He pats my arm and leaves the room.

My wife comes in with a big smile. "Now that you've provided the detective division with the information they needed and picked the culprits out of a photo lineup, there's no chance that television or the news will contaminate your judgment. You can have a TV!"

I smile a big smile. Growing up, I watched a lot of television, so it became a favorite pastime for me.

Susan turns the TV on and starts flipping through the channels, looking for something I might like. I touch her arm, and she turns around and looks at me.

I place my forefinger in the air to signal wait a minute. I cover the gauze on my throat and say, "I love you!"

She starts to cry and hugs me so hard I think I'll break. "It sounds sort of raspy," she says.

"It'll get better as the inside heals," I tell her.

We sit and hold hands. I stare at the television screen, though I'm not paying attention to the show. My mind is drifting to what I'm going to do after all this is over. *Can I stay on the job? Will I be able to work and support my wife? We bought a house two years ago. What's going to happen to that?*

My wife squeezes my hand and brings me back to reality.

I notice it's getting dark outside. "I guess you should go so you don't get stuck in the bridge traffic," I say.

She kisses me. "Okay, see you in the morning."

I lie back and watch her leave the room. I turn and look at the TV.

The new shift officer, Bill Connelly, pokes his head in the door. "Hi, Winder. How ya feeling?"

"Not bad for a shot-up guy."

"Sleep well."

I fall asleep watching TV.

★ ★ ★

I'm in a short row of men in camo utilities walking down a small, thin path. I'm the third man behind the radioman. The huge radios are worn on the back like a big pack and were equipped with whip antennas that are sometimes over ten feet long to get better reception.

As we walk slowly and quietly, the radioman doesn't notice the long piece of translucent string stretched from one branch of a tree to another, high above us. As he passes under it, the antenna snags the string, and a fragmentation grenade drops from the inside of an old C ration can that's been tied to the tree. The grenade drops down and explodes at head level, taking out the radioman and the lieutenant walking next to him, and spraying shrapnel into three more men.

I hit the ground and call for a corpsman. The rest of us fan out to protect the flanks. Loud voices mixed with screaming and the overpowering smell of the explosion invade my head, along with the many thoughts of what just happened. I'm immediately glad it wasn't me, and then I feel guilty for feeling that way. The order is given to stand up and make a small perimeter. As I move, I look down and realize that I have bits and pieces of blood and flesh stuck to me.

I move low and to the right to a better location pointing outward. I lie there and wait. We all wait. I try to concentrate on the area in front of me and watch for movement, but my mind drifts.

Our radioman's name was Steve Capps. He was from South Carolina. I was playing spades with him yesterday. I traded my C ration cigarettes with him for his can of date nut bread. Now he's gone. The lieutenant was Peter Mitchell. He came from Chicago. He was fresh out of officers' training school. That's how quickly it happens. Second lieutenants don't have much of an expiration date here.

I wonder how long it will be before I'll be able to get back and change my bloody uniform. A helicopter was called in to take the bodies back. We're given the order to slowly stand up and move forward.

I look down in the elephant grass. I see the base of a tree and try to remember that spot. I don't ever want to forget that spot.

CHAPTER 12

Healing

I wake up in my hospital room in a huge sweat. I get up, go into the bathroom, and wash my face. I come back to bed and just lie there, afraid to go back to sleep after that last dream.

It's a long night that passes slowly. I get up and walk the hallway with my escort. I never knew there was so much going on with nurses while we patients slept. They're constantly moving from room to room, taking blood and temperatures, and performing all the other duties needed to keep us well.

Morning comes, and with it comes breakfast. This is good because I'm as hungry as a hostage. I look at the tray and see oatmeal, coffee, milk, banana, apple juice, and white toast. A feast compared to the liquid antacids I've had to drink.

As I'm eating, a priest comes in. He introduces himself as Father Stephen McCoy. "Good morning, Officer. Today is Saturday. I wanted to see how you were doing and to ask, since you're Catholic, if you would want Mass and the Eucharist tomorrow."

"Yes, Father, please."

"I'll see you in the chapel at seven a.m. tomorrow then." He makes the sign of the cross over me and places his hand on mine. "Strength to you, son."

Dr. Obarto comes in early and brings with him three young men and one female. All are in white.

"Good morning, William. These are residents in training, doctors who are assisting me in my rounds this morning."

I nod hello.

The doctor starts to examine me. "We see as we remove the bandages that there is much less seepage from the wounds and that they're healing well and rapidly. The opening from the tracheotomy is almost completely closed over. The remaining pellet holes in the face and throat are getting lighter in color and are also sealing up."

"How many pellets were involved?" one of the residents asks.

"I don't remember exactly," Dr. Obarto answers. "I do know how many remain in his face and throat area."

"How many?"

"Forty-three remain inside."

"Why weren't they removed, Doctor?"

"I felt that the areas they were in caused no threat or discomfort at all, but would cause quite a bit more scarring if we removed them than we thought was necessary."

The doctor looks down at me, and I look back at him with this wide-eyed blank look on my face.

"We'll rebandage the larger incisions until tomorrow,"

Dr. Obarto says, "and then I think we can dismiss the bandages altogether and allow the wounds to start getting some air. You're healing quickly and are doing very well. Maybe in two more days, you'll be able to go home."

I nod, and they all leave the room.

Susan comes in.

"Did you hear that?" I ask.

"About you coming home in two days? That's great!"

"No, about the pellets that are still in my face and throat."

"I already knew. It was a good decision, I think. You'll never know they're there, and it cut down on the amount of scarring on your face and throat."

My thoughts go to what they might look like in there under my skin. I desperately want to look in a mirror again to see if they're still there, to see if there's been any change. I shake off the thought. I figure there will be plenty of time for looking at them later.

I slip into my bathroom to prepare for the day. I step into the shower and feel the hot water striking my body. Lathering up and rinsing makes me feel like all my problems are going down the drain. Little do I realize they're just starting.

I dry off and step to the mirror and start shaving, very carefully gliding the razor across my face and throat. As I pass the right side of my chin, I feel a tug. I look down at the razor, and I see a very small lead pellet caught between the two razor blades. I rinse the pellet off and decide to keep it. When I'm done and dressed in my pajamas, I ask the nurse for a small empty urine specimen plastic jar. I place the pellet in and close it.

Terry Moore, the driver assigned to my wife, comes into the room to see how I'm doing. A big smoker, Terry reeks of cigarettes. At the time, I was also a smoker, and the cigarette smell makes me crave a cigarette.

I look at Terry and say, "It's almost over. I'm going home soon."

"That should feel really nice."

"It seems like I've been here forever instead of just twelve days," I say. "I'll bet you'll be glad to get back to some normal routine with your family."

"Yeah, they'll be happy to see me."

While Susan and Terry leave to go get some coffee, I take a nice walk down the corridor, passing all the doors of the sick folks, Scotty at my side. "What happens to me now?" I ask.

"Well," he says, "we get you home. You get stronger. Then the job will want you to go downtown to the medical department so they can get a look at you and agree that you need to be out sick. Then at some point, I'm sure they'll want you to see a psychiatrist."

"Why?"

"They need to know how your mind is reacting to this ordeal. They want to understand how you feel, but mostly, they do it to cover their own asses."

"How so?"

"Well, they can't send you back to work if you're not a hundred percent physically and mentally healed. Otherwise, they'll be open to a lawsuit."

"Oh!"

When we get back to the room, Dr. Obarto is waiting for me. "Good morning, William. Let's take a look at you."

I sit down on my bed, and he takes my blood pressure and checks my eyes and ears. He looks at my neck wounds. "Today, we're removing the sutures." He calls in the nurse and asks Scotty to step out.

The nurse brings a tray with instruments, and the fun begins. Carefully, he snips each suture line and removes them with tweezers. I can feel each snip and each pull. Hurts like hell. As he removes each suture, he places it on the tray in gauze. I start counting them to keep my mind occupied. I also feel lucky that I wasn't awake when they put those sutures in me.

Sixty-two sutures later, he's done. He cleans off the areas with peroxide and dries them with gauze. "How do you feel now?"

"Sort of like a pincushion, but it feels good to know the sutures are out."

"Good. When you bathe, pat these areas dry. Don't rub or wipe them. Watch for signs of redness and swelling. Young man, tomorrow you may go home. I'll send along a prescription to help alleviate pain."

"I can't thank you enough, Doctor."

"You can thank me by having your wife call my office and make an appointment in one week to see me."

"Yes, sir."

When Susan comes back, she hands me a cup of coffee. It's warm and still burns slightly on the way down. I tell her the good news, and she writes it all down.

"Jane called me again yesterday and showed up this morning at the hospital crying. I sent her away like you asked."

"I'm sorry you get stuck with that job, but with all we're

going through, we don't need her drama coming in and her pretending to be concerned and making this all about her."

"Fine," she says. "I'll do what you ask."

"Thank you."

I get up from the bed, and we walk down the hallway, past the nurses' station.

All the staff smile.

We get to the window at the other end of the hall, and we look out to see all the snow on the roof and ground. I've not thought about the weather since I came into the hospital. "Do I have any warm clothes to wear tomorrow?" I ask.

"Already taken care of. They're in the closet in your room."

"Home," I say. "I never thought I'd be opening my eyes again. That night, I thought that was the end."

She looks into my eyes. "So did I. So did everyone else. What's happened to you is nothing short of a miracle." She sees that my mind is far away. "The doctor said we have to be ready by nine thirty a.m. to be discharged. He'll come in and get us."

"Okay. I'm going to Mass at seven a.m. tomorrow, and then we can pack up."

I notice a small child about four years old walk past my door. He looks in at me and smiles, then continues to walk down the hall.

I think of a night three years ago. One of the RMP (radio motor patrol) drivers called in sick. They needed an officer to partner with the driver, so for some reason, they chose me. We were making our patrol rounds, and at about

2:00 a.m., we saw a little boy around four years old walking down the street in his pajamas. We pulled the car to the curb and got out and approached the kid. We asked his name, and he said, "Leo." We asked him where he lived, and he said he didn't know. He started crying because he was confused. I gave him my handkerchief to use. We took him in the car and decided to drive him around and see if he recognized any of the houses. We drove around for two hours in the neighborhood, and nothing looked familiar to him.

Suddenly, he jumped up and yelled, "There, right there!"

We took him into the building, and he said he lived on the fourth floor. We walked him up to the fourth floor, and we saw an open door to an apartment. We knocked. No answer. We knocked again. No answer. Suddenly, little Leo pushed through the door and walked inside. We looked at each other and followed him in.

The apartment was a total mess. Dirty clothes all over, empty food cartons thrown on the floor, a heavy smell of alcohol in the air. In the living room there was a pullout couch with a man and a woman sleeping on it. They hardly had any clothes on. Leo walked past them into another room. We followed him, and he climbed onto a bed with two other children and fell asleep.

We walked back out to the living room and woke the man and woman. It took some effort. As they woke up, we tried to explain what happened and how we came into contact with Leo. They never even knew he was gone. The mother seemed very upset and apologetic. The man never did wake up enough to talk to. We said good-night and left.

All the way back to the car, we talked about how screwed up Leo's life was going to be. I realized after we left that Leo had kept my handkerchief. Since that day, I always carry two handkerchiefs.

★ ★ ★

Back in my hospital room, evening comes. I sit motionless and watch TV. I'm not even paying attention to the screen. My mind is overwhelmed with thoughts of coming home and of what's going to happen to me now. *How long will I have to stay out of work? When can I get back in uniform and get back to work? Will I ever be able to go back to work again?*

All night I walk up and down the halls, thinking. Sleep never comes. I have too much to think about, and I don't want to dream again.

Morning arrives, and I walk down to the chapel. I sit through Mass and receive the sacrament. The priest blesses me. I tell him I'm going home today. He takes my hands in his and prays that I recover and have a full life.

Back in my room, Susan is busy packing my stuff and has the clothes I'm going to wear home all laid out on the bed. With a little bit of help, I get dressed and fight with my sneakers to get them on my feet.

Dr. Obarto comes into the room, along with a nurse and a wheelchair.

"Are we ready?" he asks.

"Definitely," I reply. "Let's do like the shepherd did and get the flock out of here."

Dr. Obarto laughs and helps me into the wheelchair.

"Is this really necessary?" I ask.

"Hospital policy."

CHAPTER 13

Home at Last

As Dr. Obarto wheels me down the corridor—the same corridor I've walked probably a hundred times—all the nurses, doctors, and staff on that floor are waiting to say goodbye to me. I notice a few from the night shift have come in just to see me leave. I'm so touched, I almost lose it right there.

Susan is by my side. We get into the elevator, and as it reaches the lobby, we roll out and the entire lobby is packed with hospital staff. I wave to everybody as we move through the front doors to the street. Outside, all I can see are police officers—a sea of blue uniforms, regular officers and brass, trailing up both sides of the street, all to greet me and say get well. I imagine a few of them are amazed that I'm alive and just want to see for themselves. I've never had so much attention given to me in all my life.

Our car is parked right in front. TV crews, newspaper reporters, and cameramen are all shoving to get in close.

As I stand up, I turn to Dr. Obarto and give him a big hug. "I'll never forget you and what you've done for me," I say.

He smiles. "I should think not. I'm going to see you in my office next week."

As I bend to get in the car, my fellow officers are all patting me on the back, and bulbs from cameras are flashing in my face. I close the door, and Susan pulls away from the curb and into traffic. I try to look back to get a last glance at the hospital that saved my life, but my neck won't allow my head to turn that much because of the loss of range of motion.

All the way home, Susan holds my hand, and I stare out the car window. I roll the window down a bit so I can feel the cold air on my face. It feels so good to smell the fresh snow and trees as we drive.

"It must feel great to be out of that place and to feel the outside air again," Susan says.

I nod and keep staring. "Knowing I was coming back home to you kept me going. I never want to lose you."

She smiles and grips my hand tighter.

★ ★ ★

Susan and I pull up to our house, and there are cars all up and down our driveway. As I go to get out of the car, my nephew Tom takes my arm and helps me out. All of the family is there to greet me.

We go into the house, and everyone is so happy to see me, slapping me on the back and hugging me. I've never felt so loved in my life.

They've set up a big lunch for us all. I stick to mac salad because it's easier to eat.

Susan pours me a soda. I look at her, and she says, "Go ahead. You haven't enjoyed one in two weeks."

I take a long sip. It burns slightly as it goes down my throat, but the taste is wonderful.

We talk and talk for hours. Finally, everyone leaves, and Susan and I are alone. We have not been intimate in two weeks, and my desire to be close to her is very strong.

I slip into my sweatpants and sit down to take a break and look at all my mail. My eyes get heavy, and before I know it I am asleep in the chair.

When my eyes open again, I am in bed under the covers. I don't remember going to bed. I don't hear a sound, but the room is full of light from the windows. I get up slowly because I still get a bit wobbly when I stand. I step over to the windows and look outside. Snow covers the grass in front of the house, and it looks beautiful.

I smell fresh coffee, bacon, and eggs. I head for the kitchen, then detour to the bathroom. I look in the mirror and say to myself: *No change. I guess you are always going to be an ugly, scarred bastard. It wasn't a dream.*

In the kitchen, Susan is busy cooking breakfast. I come up from behind her at the counter and give her a big hug around her waist.

She jumps at first because I startled her, but spins around to hug me back. "How did you sleep?" she asks.

"I guess well," I respond. "I feel great. Wait a minute. I don't remember dreaming at all."

"No?"

"No! That's strange. I almost always had bad dreams in the hospital."

"Sit down and have breakfast."

Her coffee tastes great. I devour breakfast like I haven't

eaten in two months. I get up from the table and take my dish to the sink. "What now?" I ask.

"Let's just relax and spend the day together. I have to return to work tomorrow, but I want at least one day with you."

"Okay."

"The job called," Susan says. "They want you to call downtown to make an appointment with the department doctor. They also need you to call and make an appointment with their psychiatrist sometime next week. They asked that when you have the dates, you call the command, and they'll assign Terry to drive you to and from the appointments."

"Boy, they don't waste any time," I respond.

We hang out in the house most of the day. Susan spends a lot of time fielding phone calls from the newspapers, TV reporters, and well-meaning people.

The doorbell rings, and Susan's sister, Mary, is there. She's brought over fresh cold cuts and bread for lunch, and she has a big bowl of fresh sausage and peppers for our dinner. She reaches out to me and hands me a photo album. "Phil Jr. started this for you. He felt bad that you couldn't read any of the articles in the paper about you and what happened, so he started this and wants you to have it."

I take the book and open it. It's filled with what must be every newspaper article written about my shooting and the ongoing investigation, pages and pages of articles. "I don't know what to say."

She says, "I know it isn't the right feeling to have about this situation because of what happened to you, but he feels very proud of you. When you and Susan got married, none of us even gave a single thought to the fact that you might get shot on duty or come to any harm. We're all very proud of you and feel blessed that you survived."

I give her a hug. "Thank you." I sit down on the couch and start looking at the book. Phil Jr. has carefully cut out every newspaper article and picture that appeared in all the papers. Very cool. I can't believe that all these articles are about me and what happened to me.

The sisters are having lunch together at the kitchen table. The phone rings, and I wave at them that I'll answer it.

It's the press manager for the Transit Police PBA. He tells me that after I was shot and recuperating, the NYPD PBA started a bulletproof vest fund. Because the vest that I had purchased myself played such a large part in saving my life, they figured they would use my situation to start a vest fund to raise enough money to outfit all police officers with bulletproof vests.

"Well, that's a good idea, isn't it?"

"Yes, we thought it was," he says, "but we just found out that the NYPD PBA started it first, and they refuse to share any money for vests for our transit officers until every one of their ranks are fitted with a vest."

"That sucks," I say. "How many of them are there?"

"Approximately thirty thousand or more."

"How many on our force?"

"A little over three thousand," he says.

"And how about housing police?"

"About two thousand." he says.

"I don't understand that. Why don't they just give us one vest for every ten of theirs?"

"We suggested that, and they turned it down, saying their guys come first."

I was thinking to myself, *This isn't fair. They're riding on my back and using what happened to me to help their own men and not giving a thought to our men.*

He says to me, "Our PBA has decided to announce that we're instituting our own vest fund and are asking for donations."

"Well, that's good."

"We need you to make a couple of appearances to help raise money," he says.

"I've never spoken or appeared in public or in front of people before. And you want me to do it now, especially looking like I do?"

"You'll be fine," he says. "I'll let you know when all plans are solid."

"Okay," I say, still not convinced.

"Bill, we really need your help with this."

"Okay," I say.

I hang up the phone and tell Susan and Mary what I just heard. They're both shocked at the fight over the vests.

"You have to help," Susan says. "The vest saved you, and it can save others. All of you should have it. The vest should be standard issue."

I nod and walk away. I suddenly don't feel hungry. I go to the bedroom, lie down on the bed, and think about how not only are we kicked around by the public, but our own brothers in blue are turning on us. They're disregarding the fact that they're able to fulfill the need for vests because of what happened to a transit police officer. It's not fair.

As I calm down, I realize that the NYPD union is only trying to do the best for their officers. I don't blame them for thinking of their own. I might have done the same. Sleep comes quickly.

✴ ✴ ✴

I'm at 149th Street and the concourse, standing in front of a token booth with another cop, Officer Bob Somers from District 12. We're checking students who are getting out of school and trying to ride the subway home. Right in front of us, two grown men jump the turnstiles and run past us. We yell for them to stop. The guy in the lead turns and reaches for his jacket pocket. Seeing this movement, I tackle him and quickly handcuff him. I look over to see that Bobby has the second guy on the ground and is handcuffing him.

We search them both and find .32-caliber revolvers on them. As we look at each other, realizing how lucky we are to still be alive, two men come running down the subway stairs and yell to us that those two guys just robbed the bar upstairs at gunpoint. We call for an RMP to take us to the precinct so we can process the arrest. We're met there by two detectives from transit who help us with processing the guns, the money, and the arrest.

I go back to District 11, and my fellow officers are patting me on the back and saying, "Good job."

CHAPTER 14

No Longer a Police Officer?

TERRY PICKS ME UP FOR my appointment with the department doctor. We get to the doctor's office, and he calls me in. He examines me and says he's going to have an x-ray taken. When they finish, he has me step back into his office. There are books and papers everywhere.

He sits down behind his desk. "I don't know if you realize how lucky you are, Officer," he tells me. "You've undergone an unbelievable situation and have survived it. I look here at your x-ray, and I see all these little white spots that are shotgun pellets, and I'm astonished. I'm putting you on extended sick leave. If anyone bothers you about that, here's my home phone number. Call me, and I'll set them straight. You don't deserve to be harassed."

I get up to leave and shake his hand. "Thank you, sir."

"No! Thank *you*, Officer."

When we get to the car, I ask Terry if we can stop by the property clerk's office and get my personal belongings from the night of the shooting. He says yes, so we swing over. We get to the property clerk's office, and I ask for my belongings from that night. He brings out a box marked *Winder* and the date I was shot.

I open the box, and there's my blue overcoat with the top collar stays and material missing and covered in blood. I drop the coat in the garbage can. I take out my police shirt and pants. They're covered in blood as well, so in the garbage they go. I reach in and take out the vest. As I lift it up to eye level, I can see all the holes in the blood-soaked vest that haven't penetrated through. Amazing. I slowly turn and drop the vest in the garbage.

"No, that's evidence," the clerk says, so back out it comes. I reach in and take out my watch. It's also covered in blood but is still working. This I keep. I think about a popular commercial on television about Timex watches, how they take a licking and keep on ticking. I laugh to myself.

Terry and I thank the officer and start to leave to go home. On our way out, two detectives approach us and ask if we would like to hear an audiotape of the capture of the last culprit, the shooter.

"Sure," we say.

One of the detectives nods to the chief of detectives sitting at a desk nearby, and the chief explains that the two brothers, after they got into Virginia, decided to hole up in a motel. One brother decided to go out and get some food and some liquor to take back to the room. He went to an ABC store and decided to rob it at gunpoint. The state police came in and arrested him on the spot. Meanwhile, the other brother back in the room was watching television, and the news displayed his brother being escorted from the store in handcuffs. At the time of the robbery, there were twelve people in the store. In Virginia back then, that meant twelve counts of armed robbery. The brother, seeing this, decided to try and call New York and make a deal. He was switched over to the detective division. He was very upset and scared out of his mind. The conversation went as follows:

The detective tells him, "Look, the officer you shot didn't die, so we don't have a murder of a police officer to contend with. Why don't you order some food? It'll calm you down. Call me back when you're finished ordering."

The brother says okay and hangs up. A few minutes later he calls back. "I ordered pizza."

"Good," the detective says. "While it's coming, we can discuss you turning yourself in. We'll send down two detectives to bring you back to New York. You'll probably only do seven years."

On the audiotape, you can hear a knock at the door. The guy jumps up, scared, and starts yelling.

"Calm down," the detective says. "It's probably the pizza you ordered."

"Oh!" He goes to answer the door.

In the background, you can hear yelling and things smashing, followed by complete silence.

Then someone comes to the phone. "Hello, is this New York?"

"Yes, this is Detective Lopez."

"Good. This is Sergeant Maxwell of the Virginia State Police. We got your shooter in custody, and he sort of resisted arrest."

He was ultimately charged with complicity in the twelve counts of armed robbery.

I tell the detectives, "Thank you."

As we turn to leave, I salute the chief, even though I'm in civilian clothes. He stands up and salutes me back. As he does this, the whole room salutes me. Terry and I leave to head to my home.

✶ ✶ ✶

I'm sitting drinking a soda at home when the phone rings. Susan is at work, so I answer.

It's the Transit PBA press manager. "The New York, New Jersey, and Connecticut Detectives Crime Clinic Organization are having a luncheon, and they want to present you with a Cop of the Month Award. Of course, all the press will be there. Will you come?"

"Of course I will. When is it?"

"Next Tuesday at one p.m. We'll send a driver to pick you up at about eleven because it's in New Jersey. Okay?"

"Fine, but please make sure they have something soft for me to eat."

He laughs and says okay.

The luncheon goes well. I'm awarded a plaque for being the New York, New Jersey, and Connecticut Detectives Crime Clinic Cop of the Month. They make me a chopped sirloin for my lunch. Much easier to eat with no teeth. We receive a lot of press about the bulletproof vest fund and the problem between the departments. It turns out the housing police were having the same issue with the city PD.

I make a phone call to the operations desk when I get home and am given the name and number of a psychiatrist in Manhattan who is on retainer from the city and worked with a lot of cops. We make an appointment for the following Tuesday at 2:00 p.m.

★ ★ ★

I keep my appointment with Dr. Obarto, and he tells me I appear to be doing very well.

I ask him when I can expect to go back to work.

He looks at me. "I'm sad to have to tell you this, but you won't be working as a police officer much longer. Don't mention this to anyone, but they'll never be able to take you back with these injuries."

I leave his office after setting up a follow-up visit for one month later. I subsequently found out that he was a top cardiovascular surgeon, and he happened to be at the hospital that night visiting a doctor who he helped put into residence. It was karma that he was there at the same exact time I was wheeled into emergency.

Realizing that my life as a police officer is probably over stirs deep feelings inside me.

I'm asked to show up at City Hall for a meeting with the mayor. The press are all present and witness Mayor Koch presenting me with a new bulletproof vest. I promptly donate it to the transit police.

★ ★ ★

On Tuesday, I arrive at the psychiatrist's office. All around the waiting area, I see certificates hanging on the wall, showing the world the doctor's diplomas and the work he's done.

The doctor opens his office door, and I introduced myself. He tells me to sit down and be comfortable.

He's tall, about six feet three, and weighs about 180 pounds. As he shakes my hand, I notice he's right-handed. It's amazing how we're trained to always observe details. His office is painted a light blue. The carpet is a brownish color. Four bookshelves line two walls, there are two very nice lamps, and two candles are lit. I see a stack of board games and toys in the corner, for talking to kids, I guess.

"What happened to you isn't within a normal day's work," he says. "How do you feel about it?"

"I really don't know how I'm supposed to feel," I say. "Unsure, confused, pissed off, apprehensive. All of the above."

"Unsure and confused about what specifically?"

"About what's going to happen to me now. Where does my life go? If you or the department feel I can no longer function well and I lose my job, what do I do? What is my job, my goal?"

"I see. Can you tell me exactly what happened the night you were shot?"

I stare at him for a while, my palms all sweaty. Finally, I say, "I was assigned to a squad of men who handled rush-hour school arrivals and dismissals. We made sure that youth gangs from each school didn't confront each other on the way to and from school. I worked from noon to eight at night. When I was finished following the gang students, around five o'clock, I was assigned meal period. Then, after meal, I was assigned to a stationary foot post until eight o'clock. That night I was assigned to 176th Street in the Bronx, on the IRT elevated structure."

"Go ahead, continue. You're doing fine."

"I was patrolling the station, and it was almost time to return to the district. I was saying good-night to the token booth clerk to let her know I was leaving, when a young Black man came up to buy a token. He looked at me and said, 'Officer, I just walked past the bar downstairs, and I swear I saw the whole bar with their hands in the air and a guy with a gun.'

"I told him to wait there, and I yelled to the clerk to call the district and report a 10-13, officer in danger, possible bar robbery.

"I ran for the staircase leading to the street and looked out the window that was over the bar front door. I saw there was a car with out-of-state plates parked about three feet from the curb. I drew my revolver and began to descend the stairs slowly. I grabbed my radio and spoke: 'Eleven assignment number 74, requesting a 10-13 at 176th Street and Jerome Avenue. Officer in danger.'

"No response. I was constantly listening to the music in the bar. I knew that if the music got louder, it meant they were on their way out. I got to the bottom of the stairs and walked slowly to the front of the car. I wanted to catch them coming out and not inside. I didn't want a hostage situation.

"As I stood in front of the car, a man came out from the back side of the car toward the front driver door. He didn't appear to be armed.

"I yelled, 'Police! Don't move. Put your hands up.'

"He froze in place and put his hands up.

"I said, 'Lie down face-first on the ground with your arms out.'

"He complied. I started walking toward him, which gave me a view of the area under the staircase, where I saw two other men crouching down. I turned to face them with my gun aimed at them, and out of the corner of my right eye, I saw a man stick his head out of the back-seat window. I saw a huge blast. I never heard a sound."

"So you saw the blast coming?" the doctor asks.

"Yes."

"Continue," he says.

"Well, it felt like I had been burned a hundred times in a hundred places with a hot iron. It felt like being hit in the chest with a baseball bat. I felt myself rising up off the ground and being placed far back from where I had been standing.

"I lay there in such tremendous pain. I saw blood all over me and felt it coming from my throat and in my mouth. I remember one of the men yelling back as they ran away, 'Remember, man, I'm not the one who shot you.'

"I saw my .38 lying in the street, so I picked it up. I knew that if I didn't secure my weapon, the job would hit me with a dereliction of duty for failure to safeguard my equipment. I tried to aim at them and get off a shot or two, but they were already too far away. I placed my revolver in my holster. I looked up, and there was a doughnut shop in front of me. I started crawling to it and was able to stand halfway and get through the front door of the shop. As I staggered in, two men grabbed me and sat me down in a booth.

"They tried to lay me down, but I was afraid I'd drown in my own blood, so I fought with them. One of the men grabbed my radio and yelled into it that there was a cop shot and gave the address. I sat there with the blood pumping out of my neck and spraying everywhere."

The psychiatrist asks, "Are you okay?"

I'm covered in sweat, and my clothes are soaked with perspiration, but I nod.

"Take your time. Do you want some water?"

"Yes, please."

He gives me a glass of water and I continue.

"All of a sudden, two officers came through the door, picked me up, and carried me to their squad car. I found out later that they were responding to a domestic disturbance call around the corner and heard the explosion, so they came over. One of them got in the back seat with me and held my head in his lap and placed a towel to my bleeding neck.

"I kept saying, 'There were four of them. There were four of them. Please tell my wife I love her. I'm going out.' I must have passed out because I woke up on a hospital gurney being wheeled into the ER. I passed out again.

"I woke up in the emergency room with lots of yelling and doctors and nurses poking and pulling at me. When they got my overcoat off, they were amazed to see I was wearing a vest. They started cutting everything off of me and throwing it into the corner, where my friend and fellow officer, Dan Simmons, was picking up all my clothes.

"I felt my throat tightening and was finding it hard to breathe. I passed out. I woke up and was in so much pain I tried to scream, but nothing came out. I was kicking and clawing at the staff, and I looked over at Dan. He was crying

and had his head down. The doctors took a scalpel and began cutting into my throat. I started to fight again and gag. Dan ran out of the room.

"He told me later that he couldn't stand to see me in pain and bleeding like that with no ability to scream or talk. I finally passed out again, and the next thing I remember was opening my eyes in the operating room as they were operating. Just for a second. Then they yelled, and I went back under."

I stop talking and wipe my face and neck with my handkerchief.

The doctor lets me have a moment before continuing.

"Then I woke up days later in the hospital."

CHAPTER 15

Reliving the Story

THE PSYCHIATRIST KEEPS ON WRITING for quite a while, then puts his pen down, looks up at me, and asks, "Do you have a lot of dreams reliving this event?"

I nod. "And other bad dreams as well."

"From your service overseas?"

"Yes, sir."

"These dreams of the night of the shooting, are they very vivid and detailed?"

"Yes, very."

"Well, Officer Winder, the reason your dreams are so clear and detailed is primarily because you saw the blast coming at you head on. If you hadn't seen it, the reliving of the moment wouldn't be so clear."

"Will they go away?"

"I wish so much that I could tell you they will, but I sincerely doubt that you'll ever stop reliving that night, as I'm sure you must relive many of the scary situations you experienced in Vietnam. I will say that the repetitiveness and frequency of these will lessen over the years."

"I see. Not a lot to look forward to."

"You served in Vietnam in 1968, correct?"

"Yes, sir."

"That was eleven years ago. You still have the occasional dream of those experiences, don't you?"

"Yes, sir."

"But I dare say, not as often as when you first came home?"

"No, sir."

"Well, I'll stick my neck out and venture to say that these dreams will lessen in their frequency as time goes on," he says. "We're done for now. You have my number if you need to get in touch with me. I'm recommending another therapist closer to your home if you would like to continue this."

"Doctor, can you answer a question for me?"

"Go ahead," he says.

"In the hospital, I found myself crying sometimes. Now, I'm not a crier. I never cry. Can you tell me why I might be doing this now?"

"Yes, I think so. You grew up in the South Bronx, in a violent atmosphere. Yes?"

I nod.

"And you served, I understand, as a tunnel rat in Vietnam. You were wounded twice and saw many men die?"

"Yes, sir."

"You've been involved in and have seen many violent and disturbing things as a police officer?"

"Yes, sir."

"Police officers deal with and see all the terrible things in life so that the rest of us are protected from those terrible things. Well, our minds can only deal with so much. All your life, you've dealt with many things: growing up in a somewhat hostile environment, fighting overseas, being wounded, seeing atrocities very few have seen, being a police officer, and being shot on duty. When this last thing happened, with all the uncertainness of where your life was now going to go, your mind had had enough feelings and needed to spill some out. So you cried."

"Thank you, Doctor. Can you tell me what you think about my going back to work?"

"I can't tell you that. I'll submit my report to the department, and they'll advise you of their decision. In the meantime, do you need something to help you sleep?"

"Thank you, no. I don't take anything. Thank you for your time, Doctor."

"You take care, William."

As I leave his office, I realize that the candles he had burning were scented. I wonder if that was so I would feel more relaxed.

On the ride home, I stay very quiet.

My driver, Terry, looks at me and asks, "You okay?"

I nod.

"Want to go for a beer or some lunch?"

"No, please just take me home."

When I arrive home, I call the sick desk to advise them that I'm now home. Because we had unlimited sick time, when we were out sick we had to be home. If we left, it was only to go to the doctor or the pharmacy to pick up a prescription, and we had to alert the sick desk when we left the house and call to inform them when we returned home. The sick desk would then call the doctor's office or the pharmacy to check if we had gone there. They might also send a member of the department to the house to check on us.

If the condition was chronic or the situation warranted it, we were given a green dot next to our name. That meant we could leave the house without notifying the sick desk.

★ ★ ★

Three days after seeing the psychiatrist, I go back to the medical department for a follow-up checkup. Another x-ray is taken of my neck area. The doctor seems nice. He examines me and spends a good amount of time checking my scars, including the tracheotomy scar. He also checks the inside of my mouth and my teeth. He mentions the piece of the inside of my nose missing from a pellet. He checks the numbness in my neck and right thigh.

After his exam, as I get dressed, he says, "I wonder, Officer, if you realize how truly blessed you are. You've survived a terrible ordeal. Oh, by the way, when I examined you, I saw that you've lost a lot of teeth from this incident. We're going to send you to a dentist to have that taken care of. I'm also suggesting that in a couple of months you follow up with a neurologist about the numbness."

"Yes, sir."

"I understand you have parents who live in Rhode Island and that they're elderly."

"Yes, sir."

"Well, in case you might want to visit them to reassure them that you're well, I'm giving you a permit to travel out of state. It'll be noted next to your name on the sick list."

"Thank you, sir."

"Also, there are members of the department who still may want to bother you. Here's my card. On the reverse side, I'm putting my home number. If anyone bothers you about this, you call me immediately. You've gone through enough."

"Thank you very much, sir."

"You have a good day, Officer, and get well very soon."

We shake hands, and I leave.

When Terry drops me off, I think, *I love Terry. He's a great guy and a great cop, and he's a great help to me and my wife now. But man, I hate being locked in the car with him and that cigarette smell.*

Susan is still at work when I arrive home. I'm so hungry, I could take a bite out of crime, but when I look in the fridge, I don't see anything appealing. It's only eleven thirty in the morning, and I can't wait for dinner. I start remembering how a nice Italian hero would taste right about now. I decide to walk down my block to the Italian deli across the street and buy some cold cuts.

As I open the door to the deli, the owner looks up from making a sandwich. He sees me and says, "Hi, Bill." Then his face changes and he looks down.

Everyone in the store is staring at me, and when I look over at them, they all look down at their feet.

I walk up to the counter to order my food, and a little girl about six years old looks up at me and says, "Mommy, what are all those marks and lines on that man's face?"

My hand immediately goes to my neck and face, and I realize what she sees.

"Shush!" her mother says and grabs her by the hand.

I turn around, holding my neck, and walk out quickly.

I run across the street and home. Once inside, I run to the bathroom and look at my face in the mirror. Disgusted with myself, I no longer have an appetite. I go into the bedroom and lie down.

Ten million things are running through my head, all of them bad. I must have dozed off because next thing I know, it's four o'clock in the afternoon.

Susan comes home from work and excitedly tells me that she's taking us out to dinner.

"I'd really rather not go out to eat. I'm sorry."

"Why? What's the matter?"

I tell her what happened at the deli with the little girl.

"Never mind," she says. "We'll eat here."

She disappears into the kitchen, and I hear her chopping and smell the food cooking. She calls me into the kitchen.

I sit down at the table, and she places the best-looking western omelet I've ever seen in front of me. She has one for herself too.

We don't talk much while we eat. I just keep reliving the story I told the psychiatrist.

CHAPTER 16

Ceremonies and Awards Are Nice, but They Don't Pay the Bills

THE WHOLE YEAR IS FILLED with doctors' visits, dental visits, and appearing at luncheons to help raise funds for bulletproof vests for our department.

I get a call from the PBA office. They tell me that they want to set up a press conference at the hospital, where I'll present the hospital and staff with plaques to thank them for getting me back on my feet.

At the hospital, the conference room is filled with hospital staff, surgeons, fellow officers, and press. I present the awards to the staff and all the surgeons who operated on me.

In return, the hospital awards me with a copy of my x-ray mounted on a sturdy piece of wood. They also award me with a large, strong magnet for my wife so she'll always know where I am from the pellets still in my body. I think it's hilarious. I don't have the heart to spoil it all by telling them that lead doesn't attract to a magnet.

When I arrive home, I go to the mailbox to get the mail.

I receive a letter from the bulletproof vest company that says since the vest I bought from them saved my life, they're going to replace it with a new one and also provide me with a check for a hundred dollars. *Cool beans.* Don't tell anyone, but I donated the new vest to the local police department.

There are more ceremonies and awards: Cop of the Month from the Transit Police PBA, Cop of the Month from the New Jersey, New York, and Connecticut Detective Crime Clinic, an award from the Bronx and the New York Yankees. I'm invited to Yankee Stadium to present players with a plaque for coming to see me in the hospital, and on and on.

What puzzles me for a long time is that not one of my fellow officers I worked with ever come to visit me at home, even though quite a few of them live within a few blocks from me. I feel bad about that, until I realize that maybe it's because by seeing me, they will be reminded that something similar could happen to one of them.

I'm called down to headquarters to meet with the deputy chief, who informs me that my case has been before the review board and I'm going to be retired on a three-fourths pension for medical and psychological reasons.

I ask what the psychological reasons are.

The deputy chief explains that the psychiatrist said in his report that if I were placed back on patrol and had to respond to a situation that might require the use of deadly physical force, I might respond too quickly or too slowly.

On the way home, I wonder what I'm going to do now. Being a cop was my job.

When Susan comes home, I tell her, and she's very happy.

I get visits from TV and newspaper reporters at my house constantly. As I'm sitting in my living room one day, I get a phone call from a man who says he works for a morning TV show. He asks me if I would be willing to come down and be on the show to talk about the big influx of guns and crime recently. He says that the host personally asked for me.

I say, "Yes, when do they want me?"

He says that a car will be at my house at 4:00 a.m. the next Monday to pick me up. So Monday comes, and at 4:00 a.m., the car pulls into my driveway. I sit in front with the driver. When I get to the studio, they rush me into makeup. The makeup person is trying all kinds of different-colored powders to cover my neck scars. I tell her not to worry about it.

They lead me to an area offstage. I'm introduced to an officer from Texas who stands six feet tall and a police sergeant from LA County who stands six foot, two inches. They'll be on with me. We shake hands, and the show's host comes up to me to introduce himself.

He stands about six feet, four inches. "Nice to meet you," he says. "How do you feel?"

I look around me at the three hulking men. "Kind of short."

He laughs and gets down on one knee. "How's that? Better?"

I laugh and say yes.

The television interview lasts only about eleven minutes, but it's very exciting.

My retirement goes through, and I'm alerted to the fact that it's going to take fourteen months before I get my first retirement check. Also, if I take a job, I'm only allowed to make the amount that would equal the rest of the one-fourth pay I'm missing. My retirement pension is figured by my top salary at my time of retirement in 1979, which was $21,600 annually. So three-fourths of that will be $16,200 annually. Not a lot to live on, if you think about it. That leaves me $5,400 annually that I'm allowed to make if I choose to work.

As the months go by with no pension coming in, things get tight. After five months, we've depleted our savings, and our unpaid bills are piling up.

One of my friends places a call to the newspapers, and they come out and do an interview. The next day the front page of the paper reads as follows:

HERO COP RECEIVES NO PENSION
FROM THE CITY AND IS STRUGGLING.

That afternoon, I receive a call from the director of the retirement system. He apologizes and assures me that my pension check, which will include the five months of retroactive pay, will be sent right out, overnight delivery. I'm amazed at the power of the press to push people in the right direction.

Finally, there's a light at the end of the tunnel. I'll tell you one thing: all those medals, awards, and accolades are great to look at, and it's nice to admire one's accomplishments, but when you're broke and hungry, you can't boil them and eat them. Your family just stays hungry.

I receive a call from the department notifying me that I've been awarded the Medal of Honor and will be presented with it in a ceremony that happens once a year to honor all police officers who have performed meritoriously. This ceremony is called Valor Day.

The day I receive the medal, I get to see a lot of my friends from the department who are also being honored. On Valor Day, over 140 officers receive decorations for bravery. I count them all and realize that more than half of the awards are being given for actions taken by officers for incidents that happened in the street, off the transit system.

One day in summer, I get a call from a friend who is a food and beverage manager at a restaurant. "Hey, what are you doing?" He was in my academy class and was let go as part of the layoff program during the last administration.

"I'm sitting here at home watching reruns and pulling my hair out."

"How would you like to come down to the restaurant, and I'll teach you to be a line cook?"

I think about it and say, "Sure, I'll give it a try."

I tell Susan, and although she's happy I'm going to get a job, she doesn't like that I have to travel to Jersey every day.

I go for my interview and speak to my friend, and he introduces me to all the other staff. I'm started as a prep cook on days. It's very hard work, and I find I'm cutting myself and burning myself trying to keep up with the other cooks, who are culinary graduates and in their early twenties. I work hard and learn fast. In a year and a half, I'm promoted to nights, where I learn sauces and sautés. Again, I learn fast. Soon, I'm a second chef. Professional cooking is great. You make people happy, and you get to show off at home.

Restaurant life is long and tedious. You work a lot of hours and most holidays. While working, I meet some very nice coworkers. All seem to have a lot of questions about police work. I answer them as best I can.

Sadly, while I'm working at the restaurant, my father and mother pass away from heart attacks within nine months of each other.

★ ★ ★

I enjoyed my time as a cook, but I've had many different jobs after that. I really loved being a building manager.

The more I think about it, most of my jobs didn't involve me working directly with a lot of people. Another part of my PTSD.

EPILOGUE

I find myself wanting to explain to people that no matter what is going on in our lives as police officers, we have to show up to deal with the public and not let our personal life sway our opinions. I mean, think of it. You're never meeting a police officer at the best time of your life. Either you're sick and need help, are a victim of a crime, have committed a crime, or you're lost and need help. Maybe you've committed a traffic violation, or fit a description, or meet the criteria for one of the many other reasons for being stopped and questioned.

When a crime is committed, we have no other way of capturing the culprit but to stop and question people who fit the description of the assailant. It sucks, but it's the only way. It's not like we're pulling you over to tell you that we noticed it's your birthday and we have a cake for you in the trunk. No, we don't meet you at the best of times.

You lose a lot of friends when you become a cop because they know being a cop changes you. They're not as comfortable with you anymore. Everyone looks at you differently.

Also, that officer who just approached you for whatever has just occurred can be the same officer who that morning took his seven-year-old child to chemotherapy treatment. Or it could be he sat hand-feeding his seventy-year-old father who suffers from Alzheimer's disease and doesn't recognize his son anymore.

All the same problems that you all are faced with each day, we also face. But we're not allowed to show it. Yes, there are a few cops who make poor decisions. But you have people like that in every job, don't you? Think about it.

You take a person and put them through months of training, both physical and legal. You teach them how to properly use deadly physical force in a situation. You teach them come-along holds and how to properly subdue and handcuff someone. You teach them penal law; criminal procedure law; juvenile law; and alcohol, firearms, and tobacco law. You place them in a uniform with a shield that most people hate or are jealous of and expect them to make the right decision when they find themselves in the middle of a confrontation.

Police officers see the ugliest side of humanity every day. They deal with the dirt, drugs, crime, sex crimes, wife abuse, child abuse, and the inhumanity of the streets. They take the curses, bottles thrown at them, and angry people spitting on them. They get treated in a way that if it was a regular job, anyone else would walk out and quit. They brush it off, stand up, and go right back out into danger. They do this to protect and serve.

It's not the paycheck. The paycheck can never be enough compensation for what they experience each day. They do it to help. To serve. We in the force call the badge that we carry and wear on our uniform a shield because we protect you.

After a few years of working in restaurants, I was let go from the restaurant because of taking so much time off for my parents' illnesses and for their burials. I was given an excellent recommendation because they said I was a great worker and cook, but they had to hire someone while I was gone and it wouldn't be fair to ask him to leave now.

I was offered a job as a cook at New York's Rockland County Correctional Facility. I went for the interview and was hired on the spot. I must say, it felt somewhat ironic. I used to lock them up, and now I'm feeding them. How strange is that?

I have to admit when I first went to work at the jail, I had the idea that it would be like working as a police officer again. I couldn't have been more mistaken, As a police officer, I handcuffed them, transported them, processed them, and handed them over to corrections. My time with the arrestee was confined to a few hours.

As a cook at the jail, just like the corrections officers, I had no weapon, nothing between myself and the inmates. Instead of a couple of hours, I was now exposed to them ten to twelve hours a day. It's an entirely different mindset and a different kind of danger. The corrections officers are in the pod alone, with the inmates. They're forced to endure a lot of abuse from inmates.

I joined local chapter 333 of the Vietnam Veterans of America, where I met a lot of friends. Friends who had been through the same combat experiences as me. Friends who taught me about the services that were open to me at the VA.

Between my service in Vietnam in the Marine Corps and my time as a police officer, I can hold my head up proudly.

I carry a photo in my phone of the x-ray showing the forty-three lead pellets that still remain in my face, throat, and upper chest. When someone talks down about cops, I show it to people and tell them this was the extent of my commitment to the public and my job as a police officer. I stepped up. I answered the call that night and did what I was expected to do.

My reward for that was forty-three lead pellets in my face, throat, and chest, uncountable nights of nightmares and lost sleep, large scars on my throat, restricted head movement, the ability to forecast bad weather, two broken marriages, children who haven't spoken to me in over sixteen years, and the end of my career as a police officer.

My service in Vietnam and my being shot has proved a tremendous sacrifice. I'm burdened with serious post-traumatic stress disorder.

For quite a few years, I blamed myself. I never completed my twenty years with NYTPD. It was the first time that I didn't finish what I started.

Another better reward was that every law enforcement officer in this country is now issued a bulletproof vest as part of their equipment.

When I think of the officers' lives that have been saved or aided through my pain and situation, I see it as a good deal. I'm glad it worked out well for my brothers and sisters in blue. I'm proud that I had a lot to do with bringing attention to making sure that everyone in law enforcement has this protective vest. It can be hot and uncomfortable, but it works. I never took it off, not even in court.

I've worked in many fields since that night, taking jobs

as I had to in order to support myself and my family. We do what we have to do in life.

Since this incident, I have divorced again and am once again remarried. Let's pray that I get it right this time.

Please, when you see a police officer, don't immediately get the wrong impression and say, "Fuck all cops." Just feel thankful that they're there to help you. Better yet, do what I do when I see a police officer. I walk up to them, offer my hand, and say, "God bless you, Officer, and thank you. Please be careful out there." I do it because they never know if they're returning home. I didn't think I would. That's their commitment to you.

If someone called you and said, "Don't go out today; you're going to die," you'd stay home. Police officers still suit up and go out each and every day.

God bless them all.

I truly pray that you have found this book interesting. Thank you for reading it. It's taken me over thirty years to put this story to paper, but it's finally done.

Now I hope the dreams will lessen.

BACK INSIDE COVER

On a dark and freezing night, January 8, 1979, a young transit police officer patrols by himself, not knowing that in a few minutes he will experience the most traumatic and painful night of his life.

He is ever vigilant because he is patrolling alone, as all transit officers did back then. This night, the streets are solemn and very quiet. Harsh cold winds hit his face and make his eyes sting and burn.

He has one more hour till the end of shift and he can go home to a warm house, a hot meal, and a loving wife. But this officer won't be going home that night. What happens in that hour will change his life forever.

This book gives you a personal, inside view of one man's life in the New York Transit Police Department and what it cost him. You will learn that a cop's shield protects the public but not necessarily the officer.

The New York City Transit Police
Medal of Honor Circa 1980

ABOUT THE AUTHOR

William Winder was born and grew up in the Bronx area of New York City. His father came to America from Ireland, became a US citizen, and worked as a taxi driver. His mother, also of Irish descent, was from Fall River, Massachusetts. She worked as a building superintendent. William mostly attended parochial schools early on, then attended a vocational high school and studied cabinetmaking.

When he graduated from high school, the Vietnam War was in full swing, so he enlisted in the United States Marine Corps. He trained to be a rifleman and was sent to Vietnam. While there, because of his size and weight and expertise, he was volunteered to be a tunnel rat, the unofficial name for soldiers who cleared and destroyed enemy tunnel complexes.

After serving fourteen months in Vietnam, he returned to the States and served out the remainder of his time in the Marine Corps in Norfolk, Virginia, as an MP and at the Brooklyn Navy Yard as a corrections officer in the brig.

He met and married his first wife, Peggy, and soon after, they had a daughter, Elizabeth.

He took the exam for the New York City Transit Police Department and was hired in 1974. He worked in Harlem and the South Bronx area mostly, near Yankee Stadium.

After two years of marriage, he and Peggy divorced. Bill subsequently remarried twice, and it was while married to his second wife, Susan, that this incident happened.

While trying to stop a bar robbery on January 8, 1979, Bill was shot in the face, throat, and upper chest with a shotgun from thirteen feet away. He was wearing a bulletproof vest he had purchased on his own. After his shooting, the department took quite an interest in the vests, and now all officers across our great country are fitted with bulletproof vests as part of their issued equipment. William was medically retired on February 14, 1980.

While in service to the city of New York, he received two Letters of Commendation, was awarded three Meritorious Commendations, and was also awarded the New York City Transit Police Department's Medal of Honor, the department's highest award.

As a fifth-degree black belt, he studied and taught karate for over fifty-four years. He is a member of the Rockland County, Spring Valley, New York Rotary International Club.

He returned to Vietnam in 2011 and was astonished at how the country had changed. He currently resides in Connecticut with his lovely wife, Bonnie.

Printed in the United States
by Baker & Taylor Publisher Services